CityWorks

CITYWORKS

Exploring Your Community: A Workbook

ADRIA STEINBERG AND DAVID STEPHEN

THE NEW PRESS, NEW YORK

Published in the United States by
The New Press, New York

Distributed by W. W. Norton & Company, Inc., New York

The New Press was established in 1990 as a not-for-profit
alternative to the large, commercial publishing houses currently
dominating the book publishing industry. The New Press
operates in the public interest rather than for private gain,
and is committed to publishing, in innovative ways, works of
educational, cultural, and community value that are often
deemed insufficiently profitable.

www.thenewpress.com
Printed in the United States of America
9 8 7 6 5 4 3 2 1

TABLE OF CONTENTS

UNIT 1: The Individual and the Community

UNIT 2: WalkAbout the Community

UNIT 3: Contributing to the Community

PREFACE AND ACKNOWLEDGMENTS

Late one Sunday morning, the telephone rang: "They're doing CityWorks out here," said the voice excitedly at the other end of the line. It took a minute before I realized it was Gregory, a young friend who had recently graduated from the Cambridge Rindge and Latin School (Rindge), in Cambridge, Massachusetts. He was calling from Grandma's Café in Carbon County, Wyoming (population three), where he had stopped for coffee on his long drive home from a year of college in Oregon. Reading the local paper while he sipped his coffee, he had found the following item:

> CityWorks Open House Tuesday Rawlins—
> Students enrolled in the CityWorks program at Rawlins High School will host an open house on May 27 from 7 to 8:30 p.m. in the new CityWorks lab in the Occupational Center at RHS. CityWorks students will present their final projects, which were created while working in one of the 11 units that comprise the program. Students, parents, and the community have been invited to attend the open house.

Knowing that CityWorks had been invented several years earlier at Rindge, Greg was calling to let us know the amazing reach of what we had created. Laughing, he explained that Rawlins is a town of 9,000. According to "Grandma," since the uranium mine shut down and the oil boom ended the main industry of the town is the nearby "Wild Man" Penitentiary, Wyoming's biggest prison.

When a group of faculty members in Cambridge first met to design CityWorks, we had little idea how far-reaching the demand for such a course would be. The goal was to address what we saw as an immediate, local need: to create a course that would challenge students to use both their hands and their minds, to promote craftsmanship as well as scholarship. Up to this point, Rindge—like many comprehensive high schools—offered both college prepara-

tory and vocational courses, taught by different faculties, in different areas of the building, to groups of students already separated into the "college bound" and the "non-college bound." Fortunately, due to changes in the local and national policy environment, we found ourselves in a position to challenge this century-old separation of head and hand.

One key impetus was a change in the federal law governing vocational education, the Carl T. Perkins Act of 1990. With its strong call for academic and vocational integration, the Perkins Act created an opportunity to move beyond the tracking system present in most U.S. high schools. The Rindge faculty were well suited to take advantage of this opportunity: we had a mandate from Mary Lou McGrath, then Cambridge superintendent of schools, to turn vocational education in Cambridge "upside down and inside out," and a new Executive Director of Occupational Education for Cambridge, Larry Rosenstock, who had helped to draft the Carl Perkins Act.

The first step Rosenstock took was to set up a design team of interested faculty members charged with creating a new "hybrid" course that would be hands-on but not narrowly vocational. Brought in as consultants to the group, the two authors of this volume—David Stephen and Adria Steinberg—became so invested in this effort that within six months both had joined the Rindge faculty, David Stephen as the lead teacher and program coordinator for CityWorks, and Adria Steinberg as the academic coordinator with overall responsibility for curriculum and instruction at Rindge. The team began by scouring the country for ideas. Herb Kohl, a living clearinghouse for innovative curricula, provided information about a program in Los Angeles, called CityBuild, in which sixth-grade students literally created new cities, building physical models and developing the governmental and social infrastructure through role-playing and simulation. From conversations with Doreen Nelson, the founder of that program, staff members at Rindge learned of a number of other initiatives around the country, such as the Center for Understanding the Built Environment (CUBE) in Kansas City, sponsored by collaborations of architects and educators.

Another important "find" was a program called Rural Entrepreneurship through Action Learning (REAL Enterprises, Inc.) that inspired us to think about youth as an underutilized resource who could help address unmet needs in the community. In REAL, students learn that while there may not be enough *jobs* in their local area, there is interesting and valuable *work* to be done, and that they may even be able to turn that work into a vocation. And even if they cannot or choose not to, they will have learned transferable skills in the process.

The goal is to help students develop both strong roots (a feeling of connectedness to the local community through an understanding of its needs and resources) and strong wings (the knowledge and skills to succeed anywhere, rural or urban). The roots-and-wings philosophy underlies what the founder of REAL, Jonathan Sher, calls a "pedagogy of place." It is clearly applicable beyond rural communities, although the issues of community development are quite different in urban areas. In developing the CityWorks program at Rindge, we set out explicitly to discover ways to bring a community development approach into an urban vocational milieu.

This "hunting and gathering" period was very important for the design team. Although we chose in the end not to adopt any of the programs we had found, the process of talking with people and reviewing their materials helped tremendously. By the end of the three-month planning process the design team had made three key decisions:

- to create a new course, CityWorks, for all ninth-graders entering the Rindge School of Technical Arts (one of six "houses" within the high school), that would focus on teaching key applied learning skills through the lens of community development;

- to change the schedule to allow daily opportunities for the vocational and academic faculty teaching the course to collaborate on design and assessment;
- to build a new space that was neither like a traditional classroom or a traditional shop, thus using the architecture to reinforce the message that this was indeed a new kind of program.

Clearly, this was an ambitious plan. Creating a new requirement for students in an already crowded high school curriculum involves eliminating something else—in this case a century-old tradition of having freshmen in the vocational program do an "exploratory," in which they sample all of the "shops" offered in the school before selecting a vocational major, and presumably, a lifelong career. For the vocational faculty, the "exploratory" represented an annual opportunity to recruit students for their programs, which, in turn, was connected to their sense of job security. Acutely aware of the trend towards declining enrollments in vocational education, a critical mass of the faculty were willing to take a chance on forging a new direction.

With this increased support, the design team moved into an "if you build it they will come" phase of development. Moving the electrical shop to a smaller room gave us a large space to work with—no small feat in a hundred-year-old building in which space was at a premium. David Stephen, an architect by training, suggested we borrow the notion of "studios" from design schools, subdividing most of the room into small spaces, each with its own worktable and locked cabinet for hand tools and art supplies. This arrangement would make it possible to create small teams, with the flexibility to regroup as a project necessitated. A large open area at one end of the room with large movable display boards would be used for gatherings of the whole class as well as public events such as presentations and exhibitions. The CityWorks room was truly a space designed for collaborative, productive work.

With its unique space design and an unusual teaching force of vocational and academic faculty, paraprofessionals, and bilingual specialists, City-Works became a "signature" course for Rindge. A hybrid of academic and vocational education, in which key academic and vocational competencies and personal qualities were explicitly modeled and taught, it was a central experience around which faculty came together. The daily CityWorks meetings not only gave faculty an arena for assessing students' strengths and needs, but it also allowed faculty members to view one another as adults with expertise to share. In short, it began to change the conversation in the school.

Caught up in our own intense process, we were pleasantly surprised to discover the potentially widespread appeal of the central ideas of the CityWorks program. This appeal began to be evident soon after the program's initiation. After just one year, City-Works received a Ford Foundation Innovations Award in recognition of the program's groundbreaking effort to "change the purpose and content of vocational education."

Soon after, we found ourselves entertaining a steady stream of visitors from other schools, one team of educators coming from as far as Utrecht, in the Netherlands, to study and adapt the CityWorks approach. Over the years, various faculty members have presented and given workshops at dozens of conferences, including the Hands and Minds conferences co-sponsored by Rindge and the Center for Law and Education. Somewhere along the line, a teacher from Rawlins, Wyoming, had probably attended such an event and left with a draft of the ever-evolving lessons, units, and projects and perhaps even a blueprint of the unusual space design of the CityWorks room. With the publication of this book, the full CityWorks curriculum will finally become available to anyone who wants it, rather than those who happen upon a "bootleg" copy. We are very grateful to Ellen Reeves, our editor at the New Press, and to the Pew Charitable Trusts for making this possible. We would like to thank Hilary Goldhammer, staff writer for the Big Picture Company in Cambridge, Massachusetts, for her assistance on the Resource Guide and Work-Log reflections. We would also like to thank our friend and colleague Larry Rosenstock, now principal of High Tech High School in San Diego, California, whose vision, leadership, and enthusiasm propelled the restructuring of the Rindge School of Technical Arts and the creation of the CityWorks program. We also remember, with love and gratitude, the hard work of scheduling, scrounging supplies, and protecting the space for CityWorks of Anthony Carnabuci. Finally, we would like to acknowledge the many Rindge teachers who taught CityWorks and worked on its development over the years, as well as the loaned employees from the Polaroid Corporation who became valued members of the team: Richard Barbosa, Marcus Bell, Francesca Bini, Tony Carnabuci, Roy Carter, Serafim da Cunha, James DeLena, Brad DeRocher, Philip Dussault, Manny Goncalves, David Goodwin, Joel LeGault, Tom Lividoti, Rich McDonald, Ingrid Motsis, Albert Newton, James Ravanis, Ken O'Brien, Fred Peary, Rich Petrillo, Tony Russo, John Shea, Gilberto Sosa, Terry Stewart, Alfred Stowell, George Traganos, Acloque Wakintses, Paul Walsh, and Rosalie Williams. Special thanks to Tamara Berman for contributing several activities in Unit 1.

THE COMMUNITY AS TEXT
An Overview of the Cityworks Curriculum

The CityWorks curriculum outlines ways to engage teenagers in an exploration of the needs and resources of the community in which they live and go to school. In a sense, the community is a "text" that students learn to read. First by pooling their own knowledge and experiences, and then by venturing out on expeditions, they collect information on the neighborhoods, systems, people, and industries that surround them. Back in the classroom, students go through a process of representing and analyzing aspects of the community they have documented. Finally, each group of students adds its own chapter to this ever-evolving "text"—proposing changes in or new designs for their community and presenting these visions to community planners, neighborhood associations, and other audiences of adults who live and work in the area.

In part, the work of CityWorks is "hands-on," involving the creation of artifacts and exhibits through which students bring what they are learning about the city back into the classroom. Students take photographs and produce videos, make maps and models, write oral histories and brochures. In other words, they use a variety of materials and tools of artistic and technical domains. But the artifacts students create are not an end in themselves. For example, in one project students paint a wall map of the city that they wire to light up selected landmarks. The process of placing various landmarks on the map opens the door to social analysis.

Students might begin to consider questions such as: Where are the teen centers? Why do they remain largely racially segregated? Will the new one the city is proposing solve this problem? Where could the community locate a teen center in order to attract youth from all ethnic and racial communities of the city? At this point, work happening inside the classroom becomes relevant and potentially helpful to a larger community. For example, a citywide teen council or the mayor's office would be an appropriate audience for a CityWorks proposal for a new multicultural teen center.

Ultimately, the goal is for students to develop and share their own visions of their community, both as it is and as it could be. The expectation is not that all of the new buildings or parks they propose will be built, or the services they plan will be offered, but rather that their work will be taken seriously as a valuable contribution to ongoing dialogue about improving the quality of life in the community. Genuine adult interest becomes the standard by which students and teachers select problems and projects that are "real enough" to be worthy of inclusion in CityWorks.

Academic and Vocational

In asking students to use both their hands and their minds, CityWorks addresses a bifurcation in the high school curriculum (and student body) that has existed for nearly one hundred years. Observing CityWorks students at work on a project, visitors often note that it is impossible to tell whether the setting—or the students—are academic or vocational. In crossing boundaries of departments and disciplines, and with its focus on community development, CityWorks stands out from the other offerings in a typical high school course catalogue—a departure from the usual in both approach and content.

Like vocational education, CityWorks is hands-on: using a variety of tools, materials, and technologies, teams of students work on products intended for use by real clients. Unlike traditional vocational education, however, the purpose of this productive effort is not to select and train for a particular trade. In exploring the life and work of their community, CityWorks students are expected to use their minds in ways traditionally associated with rigorous academic course work. Students learn to do interviews, collect oral histories, and conduct research in local archives; they grapple with how to represent complex ideas to a variety of community audiences—in written form but also orally and visually, through two- and three-dimensional modeling.

CityWorks offers an action laboratory setting for applied learning. Over the past half century of American education, the term "applied" has become synonymous with watered-down academics, offered to reluctant or resistant students as a substitute for the college preparatory curriculum; and "academic rigor" has become equated with the coverage of increasingly more abstract topics or concepts. In contrast, the point of CityWorks is to offer students an opportunity to engage in learning experiences which are both rigorous *and* applied. It is an attempt to teach craftsmanship without a particular craft or trade outcome in mind and an attempt to foster the disciplined inquiry of scholarship without covering a set group of topics and content material. Students write and create visual displays, which they present orally to real audiences. They apply mathematical concepts to the construction of scale models and to mapmaking. In other words, students participate in increasingly sophisticated applications of relatively basic skills. CityWorks is not about accumulating more and more facts or "covering" more subject matter, but about using (and hence sharpening) the skills and understandings which are fundamental to performing well in academic, community, and work settings. In this way, CityWorks can be of benefit to a full range of students, from the most to the least academically avid.

Mastering the New Basics

Doing well in school usually involves learning to answer questions and carry out assignments made by the teacher, and, most importantly, coming up with correct responses on tests—usually in artificial situations in which students are expected to work alone, without reference materials, tools, or technology to aid their thought. Doing well in *life* requires a very different set of skills—framing questions, planning, organizing, finding and analyzing information, working with others, assembling key resources and tools, testing out ideas, and trying again.

CityWorks is an attempt to address the disjunction between school and the "real world"—a disjunction that leads many students to wonder why they are in school at all. The projects are not simply an extension of the curriculum or a way to assess learning, they are central to instruction. As in a workplace, students are expected to be productive and create high-quality work.

Asked to propose designs for a neighborhood in the process of revitalization, or to design exhibits for a new heritage museum, students need to become flexible and creative thinkers and problem-solvers, who understand the value of collaboration and can communicate well with various audiences. Successful completion of these projects requires flexible thinking, teamwork, time and resource management, problem-solving, and public presentation.

This skill set empowers young people to become good students and good community members as well as productive and professional workers. As long as employers required schools only to turn out docile workers, capable of carrying out routine production processes, the democratic vision of an educated, questioning citizenry remained in conflict with the economic and vocational purposes of schooling. Today, business leaders make policy statements on education that are remarkably similar to those of university scholars—both groups calling for high school graduates who have learned how to frame and address semi-structured or unstructured problems and to carry out complex multi-step projects.

Joining Adult Conversations

For many students, CityWorks may be the first time since third or fourth grade in which they are given time during the school day to work on a project. Similarly, it may be the first time since elementary school that the focus of the curriculum is on the community. Community studies, if found at all in American schools, usually appears as social studies units in the first or second grade. In fact, the traditional social studies sequence proceeds from the more to the less familiar. By the middle or upper elementary grades, units on family and neighborhood give way to studies of Egypt or Greece. Often, this shift also implies a move away from active exploration and hands-on learning to more "bookwork" and written products.

The point of CityWorks is to take advantage of something familiar and accessible—the community in which students live and go to school—to engage students in solving authentic problems and fashioning useful products, activities they do not often get to do in their studies of distant times and cultures. Cognitive scientists such as Howard Gardner and Lauren Resnick define intelligence as the ability to solve problems and create products, emphasizing that intelligence cannot be considered apart from the purposes for which it is used.

Community problem-solving is an important arena in which students learn to use their intelligences in different ways and to develop the types of expertise that will be recognized as valuable by adults. If teachers want students to take the work of learning seriously, it is imperative to show them that there are adults outside of school settings doing similar tasks, thinking through similar kinds of problems, who take student work seriously. Students today have few opportunities to work alongside or even interact individually with adults. They spend most of their time in school, part-time jobs, and extracurricular activities—age ghettos in which they are surrounded by peers and vulnerable to peer pressure. Although adults may play important roles in each of these settings, their roles do not always encompass forming real relationships with the young people in their charge.

A key issue for high schools in recent years has been the difficulty of ensuring that each student be known well by at least one adult. Although an important goal, it is only one part of addressing the need adolescents have for connection with adults. Teenagers also need to feel that their voices—individually and collectively—are heard and valued by the adults around them and that they can contribute to important conversations in this community.

Making a Difference

For the most part, what students do in school is dissociated from the life and work of the community in which they live. Unlike the last century, when young people participated in the farming, small businesses, and trades of their family and neighbors, the work of adults is no longer visible to students. There are few if any opportunities to work alongside adults or to be taken seriously in an enterprise worthy of adult concern. By focusing on the community, teachers and students can find a ready source of issues and problems that adults perceive as important but do not necessarily have the time or resources to address.

"Field studies" is the term popularized by Charles Jett, a Wheaton, Illinois consultant, to describe student projects originating from local businesses or community leaders. As Jett notes: "The city managers' desk has two major piles—one pile consists of the projects that must be attended to immediately, the other are things that should be addressed, but are politically or socially less urgent." This second pile is a great source of problems around which to formulate projects appropriate for CityWorks students.

Of course, such projects are not necessarily of immediate relevance to teenagers. Asked to identify what they consider to be the "top ten" issues affecting them, most teenagers will start with topics such as AIDS, teen pregnancy, or violence, not issues of city planning or development. The main overlap with lists made by adults in the community is in the area of public safety. But this is as likely to be a matter of contention between adults and young people as a potential area of commonality. Many adults see teenagers as part of the problem rather than an underutilized resource that could be mobilized to improve the quality of life in the community.

In a study of community youth organizations that work effectively with economically disadvantaged young people, Shirley Brice Heath and Milbrey McLaughlin came to the following conclusion: "The youth organizations that attracted and sustained young people's involvement gave visible and ongoing voice to a conception of youth as resources to be developed and as persons of value to themselves and to society." It is exactly this message that CityWorks tries to convey.

The message is most likely to be heard by the students if it comes not simply from a teacher but from a broader group of community members. It is important from the beginning to bring in a variety of adults, with different experiences and expertise. Planners from the city's community development department can use their slides and maps to take students on a virtual tour of the city, outlining major aspects of life and major issues affecting the quality of life for citizens of different ages and backgrounds. Neighborhood activists can walk students through an area of the city plagued with lead paint or other environmental hazards. Graduate students in design at a nearby university can describe their own efforts to design new parks or redesign old subway stations and enlist the teenagers to help them in these efforts.

Even if the issues outlined by such visitors do not seem of immediate relevance to students, the very fact of adult interest and participation has an important effect—especially if these adults treat them as people who have important prior knowledge and experience to bring to bear. Students then begin to feel that what they know and what they bring to this work matters. Equally important, when adults from the community bring their expertise into the classroom, they also bring a sense of passion and mastery too often missing in school. Students find out about challenges experienced by adults as they go about their daily work and lives.

Community adults also help to raise the standards for student work. Looking at student products and performances through trained eyes, they help young people see that there are different standards of performance and products in different domains. As they carry out their presentations and exhibitions, students gain a better understanding of what is considered quality work. Encouraged to look inward to set their own personal standards, they then have the opportunity to hold their own standards against those of the school and those of "real world" experts.

Ultimately, the purpose of CityWorks is to help students develop the sense that life outside of school is a legitimate area of inquiry inside the classroom and that course work can meet real needs. When this happens, students begin to see themselves as people who can have a positive effect on their community— from their own small peer group to the many students, families, adults, and organizations that comprise the school and its surrounding neighborhoods. Most importantly, they come away with the sense that their contribution is both needed and valued.

The Contents of This Book

The activities and projects described on the following pages lay the groundwork on which young people, and their adult guides and mentors, can create their own version of CityWorks, customized to the particular needs and resources of their own school and larger community. Unit 1, The Individual and the Community, serves to acclimatize students to an unusual learning environment by providing an explicit introduction to the six CityWorks Goals:

1. **Communicating Well**
2. **Working as a Team**
3. **Producing High-Quality Work**
4. **Using Math, Measurement, and Fundamentals of Design**
5. **Using Problem-Solving Skills**
6. **Knowing the City's Resources and Needs**

Students come to internalize these goals, and set some of their own, as they proceed through a series of activities and experiences—from developing their own personal statements on video and writing biographies of one another to creating three-dimensional models of real and fantasy landmarks and placing these on a giant map of their city. In the units that follow, the CityWorks goals provide a framework for ongoing student reflection on their activities and accomplishments in the course.

Unit 2, WalkAbout the Community, begins with home teams of students selecting a theme or issue in their community that they want to investigate. It is their job to identify particular people and sites that will offer important information to their inquiry and to plan a visual and oral presentation for an audience of peers and adults. In the process, students hone their investigative and presentation skills. They learn the value of seeing the familiar through new lenses and how much can be revealed by framing new questions and documenting information in various media.

Taken together, these first two units afford students an apprenticeship in doing projects. These relatively short-term projects involve teamwork and communication in tackling problems that do not necessarily have a right answer. Students practice the competencies and skills that educators, community, and business partners all identify as being critical for success in school and beyond, doing so in the context of addressing real issues and creating products and presentations. These opening activities are also structured to encourage particular behaviors and dispositions central to success in school and beyond—these include persistence, flexibility, and the disposition to try new things and learn from mistakes.

By the completion of the WalkAbout unit, students have learned to "read" their community and have the skills—both individual and group—to do so. The culminating unit, Contributing to the Community, offers students the opportunity not only to study but also to contribute their own designs and ideas to a current community development issue. They may, for example, become involved in a neighborhood revitalization campaign, an effort by the local historical society to create a new discovery museum, or a problem of environmental pollution.

Here, the text offers both templates and examples from actual CityWorks classes, in the spirit of suggesting directions the class might want to take. Finally, the curriculum provides information to guide students, teachers, and community members in creating their own culminating exhibition and open house, an event which highlights for all the scaling of the wall between the school and the community.

NOTES TO THE TEACHER
MAXIMIZING LEARNING

The Teaching Team

CityWorks is not just a different learning environment for students, but a new teaching environment for adults. It is unlikely that any individual teacher will feel comfortable leading all of the activities and projects of CityWorks. For example, a task such as building scale models will be much easier for a drafting or design teacher to supervise than for most academic teachers, but the drafting teacher might feel much less comfortable than a language arts teacher in helping students with their writing, and a social studies teacher might feel most at home with facilitating an assessment of community needs.

The course works best when the teaching staff takes a team approach, with different teachers leading different projects and/or when a range of community experts and resource people are brought in to help with particular activities (see below for a further discussion of bringing in community experts). Because CityWorks asks students to use both their hands and their minds, it is best if the teaching team includes people with technical and artistic as well as academic backgrounds.

It is certainly possible for one teacher to take the lead, as long as that person has the support and time to work outside his/her own comfort areas. The course itself can also be modified according to the strengths of the teacher(s) who are offering it as well as to the expertise of outside resource people who are available to help.

Student Teams

Many of the activities and projects of CityWorks work best if they are completed by a team of students working together under the guidance of an adult. At the beginning of the year, students can be assigned to "home teams," each of which has a designated area or studio within the CityWorks room (see Space, below). This is the team within which students do introductory activities relating to the goals of communicating well and working as a team. Students stay in this team for the WalkAbout Project, working together to identify a theme that interests them, then subdivide further to carry out the work. As students move into the Community Development Project, they choose new teams based on their particular area of interest and the kind of product they want to develop.

Ideally, teachers are teamed (see above) in such a way as to make the student-teacher ratio in CityWorks no greater than 10 to 1, which is, of course, much lower than most academic courses. If there is an adult for every 8 or 10 students, students will be able to work productively—with adequate guidance and supervision—in small project teams of 4 or 5. Certainly, it is not easy to achieve this ideal ratio. Some of the strategies schools use include

- limiting the number of vocational electives to allow technical/ vocational teachers to work in the CityWorks environment;
- enlisting the help of paraprofessionals; e.g., teacher aides or bilingual assistants;
- making CityWorks an inclusion model and hence enlisting the help of special support staff; e.g., special education tutors;
- convincing a partnering business to give an employee release time to help out in CityWorks; and
- assigning student teachers to CityWorks.

With any of these strategies, there is a primary teacher responsible for the course who organizes and orchestrates the other adults.

For certain projects, the student teams will also need the assistance of community experts. These adults will not be asked to make as much of a time commitment. Rather, their role is to come in for specific functions (e.g., presentations, assessments) or to provide more intensive assistance during defined time periods (e.g., during the community development project). The functions of these adults, and strategies for recruiting them are described below.

Community Experts

In CityWorks, students identify and address problems that are of interest and concern to a variety of people in their community. The subject matter and activities of the course provide opportunities, not present in many classrooms, for students to learn from and alongside adults other than a designated teacher. To take advantage of this opportunity, school staff need to reach out to the community, find out who has relevant expertise or experience to share, and enlist the support for the program.

The course comes alive when students have the opportunity to interact directly with neighborhood activists, local businesspeople, graduate students in urban planning, and public officials and public employees, especially those involved in community development and planning. These adults can help in a number of ways—by giving presentations, listening and responding to students' ideas, acting as interviewees or informants, guiding students in the creation of project ideas, and assessing the completed work. Their interest in what students are doing helps students feel that their work is important and useful. The expertise that these adults can bring also adds tremendously to the teaching resources for the class. The teacher does not have to "know it all." This places the teacher in the very different role of not simply acting as a purveyor of information or assessor of students but as a facilitator and orchestrator of the learning environment.

While having other adults contribute to the teaching can be very helpful to CityWorks teachers, it is also true that arranging for this type of ongoing connection with the community can be difficult for teachers. The classrooms where teachers spend most of their day do not ordinarily have phone lines or voice mail. In many schools there is no reliable system for getting messages. One possibility is to enlist the help of a school volunteer or of a university intern who can make this work part of a school project of his or her own. Another solution is for one member of the teaching team to have a lightened teaching load in order to do the outreach and take care of the overall management of the program. The important thing is to find some way to connect students to adults in the community, without overburdening the classroom teachers.

At particular times in the year, it will be especially important for students to be coached and mentored by experts—most notably during the community development project. To be productive and produce high-quality work, each small group of students will need some guidance from an adult who has experience developing the type of final product (e.g., a business plan or an architectural scale model) the team has selected. One way to address this need is to develop a relationship between the CityWorks course and a local graduate program in design, urban planning, or education. This works best if a professor at the university agrees to accept as a project for his/her course the work the graduate students do to help Cityworks students complete their community development projects.

Why Projects?

In the course of their careers in the American schools of today, most students take hundreds, if not thousands, of tests. They develop skill to a highly calibrated degree in an exercise that will essentially become useless immediately after their last day in school. In contrast, when one examines life outside of school, projects emerge as pervasive. Some projects are assigned to the individual, some are carried out strictly at the individual's initiative, but most projects represent an amalgam of personal and communal needs.
—Howard Gardner, *The Unschooled Mind*

CityWorks is a project-based course. Students learn through participating in extended projects focusing on life and work in their community. The project provides a context for learning important skills: how to frame a question or problem, how to draw on multiple sources of information and in particular on community expertise, and finally, how to present findings. Assessment is ongoing; rather than reproducing what they know on a test, students reflect on what they are learning, submit their work for peer and teacher review, and ultimately produce exhibitions for a community audience.

The reliance on project-based learning, and particularly on field-based investigation, sets City-Works apart from most high school courses. Beyond third or fourth grade, projects are a relatively rare occurrence in school. Concerned about the pressures of time, teachers often rely on what they perceive as more efficient ways to cover the material: comprehension questions, quizzes, essays, recitations, and tests. When projects are assigned, for example, a final paper for history or an experiment for the school science fair, students are usually expected to do the work outside of school, with only their parents to help them move through a complex and perhaps ambiguous set of tasks.

Teachers, particularly in high school, do not see it as their role to teach students how to do a project. Yet this may be one of the most important sets of skills students could learn in school. Increasingly, the health of our communities depends on the active participation of citizens who make it their "project" to improve various aspects of life in their neighborhood. Asked what they look for when they hire and promote, employers also list skills associated with project-doing: communication, working well in a team, and solving semi-structured problems.

Creating a Culture of Quality

Exemplars. The culture of many classrooms is to get by with as little as possible. Doing the minimum is the accepted way. It is very important in CityWorks to change classroom culture to one in which a standard of productive effort and professionalism prevail. One of the most important things a teacher can do to create a culture of quality is to show students exemplars of finished work. Whenever possible, these examples should be drawn from the best student work of the previous years: exhibition boards, student writings, and videos of student presentations.

Whether or not the work of previous students is available, it is important to bring students into contact with adults who do this kind of work, and to bring professional standards to it. Presentation boards are fairly standard practice in graphic design, architectural, and advertising firms. Although the presentation boards brought in by visiting designers may not contain the same elements as those required in the CityWorks curriculum, they will model a standard of professionalism, and the designer can talk with the students about what makes a good visual display and how to think about the balance of image and text. If possible, the visiting designer could return when students are in the process of assembling their boards, to provide feedback, and finally, attend an exhibition of the finished work.

Knowing exactly what kinds of work products are due helps students to plan and be productive throughout the process of doing the project. Another useful device is the setting of checkpoints before the final deadlines so that students can get feedback while there is still time to improve on their work.

Work Requirements. When the forms of the work products required are unfamiliar to students—such as the use of a presentation board as a visual aspect of their exhibition—even more structure may be needed. For example, the first time students put together a presentation board (e.g., Unit 2, Group Neighborhood Presentation Board and the Focus Theme Presentation Board), it is a good idea to specify what types of material should go on the presentation boards and even offer a sample layout. Sometimes in the name of allowing space for creativity, teachers are reluctant to be explicit about the criteria for good work. Then students find themselves graded down for "sloppiness" inattention to detail, or not including a particular topic or theme. By studying a template, all students will know what elements are required.

How Good Is Good Enough? Knowing what's required is different from knowing what constitutes high-quality work. One way to make more transparent the criteria on which the work will be evaluated is for the class to work together on developing a standard for assessing the quality of each element.

For example, if photographs are a required element of the presentation board, the class, using a scale of 1 to 4, might decide on the following criteria for assessing the use of photographs: photographs not in focus, not clear how they relate to the theme, rated 1; photographs in focus, but not clear how they relate to the theme, rated 2; sharp, clear photographic images that correspond to interviewees, sites visited, etc., rated 3; photographs arranged to tell a visual story and pick up on themes of the board, rated 4. If the class creates such a standard for each element, students will have a clear sense of what it means to produce high-quality work.

Habits of Reflection: WorkLogs and Portfolios

In its focus on community issues and its emphasis on active exploration, CityWorks bears a closer resemblance to the kinds of youth activities, projects, or clubs that engage students outside of school than to traditional academic courses. By bringing such experiences inside the school, CityWorks affords an opportunity for students to become more cognizant of their own interests and strengths and, in the process, develop habits and skills that can help them become lifelong learners.

The challenge for CityWorks teachers is to encourage students to develop an internal sense of the standards for good work. This is not likely to happen as long as schoolwork remains disposable, something one does only for a grade and then discards. From the beginning of the year, it is important for students to become interested—and ultimately invested—in assembling a portfolio of their work, which includes not just the products they make but ongoing written reflections and self-assessments.

After each major activity in the curriculum, students reflect on what, how, and where their learning took place. CityWorks writing exercises take two forms: WorkLog reflections and Portfolio Record forms. WorkLog reflections encourage students to think and write about CityWorks activities and projects in terms of the broader issues and ideas that they evoke. Portfolio Records are more descriptive of the actual project the student has been working on, the process they went through to complete it, and how they would assess their work. The writing that students do for both WorkLog reflections and Portfolio Records can be free-form (see page 187–188 for the template) or in response to the prompts provided within the units. Because much of the work in CityWorks is visual and hands-on, forms are provided that contain space for a drawing or a photograph as well as writing. Reluctant writers in particular find it helpful to begin by describing what they have made before reflecting on the process of creation.

The WorkLogs are an important part of the student's portfolio, enabling the reader (and the student) to understand what was in the student's mind as he/she did the work. In assembling their portfolios, students are also asked to think about how their various projects relate to the goals of CityWorks. If learning to use a design process to solve problems is an important goal of CityWorks, where does this show up in the student's actual project work?

In Unit 1 (The Individual and the Community) students spend time actually creating a storage case for their portfolio. This, then, becomes the case within which they keep their writings, drawings, photographs, disks, and videotapes. The process of making the portfolio case is both an exercise in measurement and design and a reinforcement of a basic CityWorks message: that what you create matters and is worth saving. It is important to reinforce this message periodically throughout the year, giving students opportunities to add to, organize, and share their portfolios and eventually to ask them to use it as the basis for a final reflective essay.

Space

The small desks and cramped quarters of the traditional classroom may be adequate for individual reading and writing work, but they do not lend themselves well to group problem-solving, the creation of visual displays and models, or the exhibition and presentation of student work. The room used for CityWorks should be part academic classroom, part art room and part vocational shop.

Another image that it might be helpful to keep in mind is that of the flexible and modular arrangements in high-performance work settings where people work both individually and in small teams to tackle problems and invent solutions.

For students to work productively on the design projects of CityWorks, they will need to sit at worktables or workstations where they can spread out their work and which accommodate meetings of small design teams. It is also important to have an area of the room available for larger presentations and exhibitions of student work.

Materials and Tools

Many of the activities of CityWorks depend on the visual representation of ideas in two-dimensional displays and three-dimensional models. To create such displays and models, students will need access to appropriate materials and tools, ranging from presentation boards to high-quality markers, from mat knives to computers equipped with software applications such as Power Point and Quark. (Lists of materials and tools accompany each unit.)

If students are expected to do high-quality work, they need the kinds of materials and tools that craftspeople and professionals use. Such materials, of course, will not be in unlimited supply. One of the valuable lessons students learn is how to plan ahead and use materials creatively and wisely. Such planning is an important part of the design process.

It is also important to have safe storage for tools and materials and for students' works-in-progress. Students become frustrated when tools are broken or missing, and there is nothing worse than students finding that their work has been destroyed through the carelessness of others. It is important to take the time early on in the course to establish a system for keeping track of and sharing materials and tools and protecting student work. At the least, it will probably be necessary to have a locked storage area, with small groups or teams responsible for their own materials within this area. The issues are, of course, similar to those in any art room or vocational shop. Teachers from those departments can be very helpful in sug-

gesting ways of encouraging appropriate work habits and of managing the situation.

Resources

Setting up the CityWorks room and keeping the students supplied with the materials they need for their design projects costs money. One way to defray these costs is to engage in local fund-raising from corporate and community partners. CityWorks is a course that can attract support from such partners, who understand the need for students to learn the kinds of skills that CityWorks teaches. Such agencies and organizations sometimes have exactly the right kinds of materials and equipment to donate to the course. For example, the CityWorks program at the Rindge School of Technical Arts in Cambridge, Massachusetts, was able to obtain substantial donations of film from the Polaroid Corporation and received software as well as computers from other local companies.

Nearby colleges or universities are an important source of human resources. Undergraduate or graduate students seeking internships or doing field studies can be extremely valuable in everything from setting up community contacts to mentoring small teams of high school students as they proceed through the steps of a community development project.

Using the CityWorks Curriculum

The pages that follow contain materials for the teacher and for the student. (Pages will be labeled to indicate the intended audience.) Each of the three units begins with a listing of all of the activities of the unit, and an introduction for the teacher that frames the purposes and approach of these activities. (On pages 176-183 teachers can find a complete listing of the materials, tools, and handouts required to carry out each activity, as well as an approximation of the time the activity will take.)

The bulk of the material that follows is designed to be copied and handed out directly to the students. Each unit contains a number of suggestions for Work Log reflections and Portfolio entries. To do this writing, students will need copies of the Work-Log Reflection Form and Portfolio Record Form provided on pages 36 and 37.

UNIT 1

The Individual and the Community

Goal 1
Communicating Well

Goal 2
Working as a Team

Goal 3
Producing High-Quality Work

INTRODUCTION FOR THE TEACHER

The activities of this first unit serve both to introduce students to the goals of CityWorks and to acclimatize them to a new kind of learning environment. In a course that is nontraditional in its content, style of teaching and learning, and even in its physical space, it is especially important to send students clear signals early on about what to expect and how to behave.

Certainly many high school courses begin with the teacher sharing the goals. But too often students play a passive role, without much of a context for making sense of the "big picture" that the teacher might be offering. And this may be the only time during the semester that students hear a description of what the course is about or why it might be important.

In this first unit of CityWorks, students not only hear about the goals of the course but engage in activities that make each of the goals concrete. In the process, students also begin to practice many of the skills, personal qualities, and habits of mind that CityWorks is designed to teach: teamwork, individual and group presentation, persistent striving for high-quality work, reflection, and problem-solving. Underlying CityWorks is the assumption that it is important to be explicit with students about all of these aspects of what they are expected to learn and that being explicit means demonstrating rather than simply telling students what the course is about.

In addition to helping students begin to trust and feel comfortable with others in their home team, Unit I introduces the WorkLog, the portfolio, and the presentation—basic rituals of participation throughout CityWorks. Writing entries in the log, collecting samples of their work for their portfolios, and making presentations to and receiving feedback from the class (and ultimately, other audiences) will be the key ways that students reflect on and assess the learning experiences of CityWorks.

Goals 1 and 2: Communication and Teamwork

The first two goals of CityWorks: Communicating Well and Working as a Team, lend themselves to activities in which students learn to reflect on themselves as learners and group members, listen carefully to one another, and present ideas and information in a variety of formats (written, visual, and oral). Because these two goals are so closely related to one another, it is possible to combine the activities, mixing and matching in whatever way works well for a particular group of students.

For example, a team game, like the name game, might provide a level of interaction and fun that helps motivate students through the sustained individual work required to complete a partner biography or resumé. In selecting among these activities, the teacher should pay attention to pace and variety. Ultimately, the important thing is for students to learn one another's names (surprisingly often this does not occur in many classes), to develop habits of reflection, and to begin to trust one another enough to share ideas and information freely.

Goal 3: High-Quality Work

Students are used to thinking of their schoolwork as something that only the teacher cares to review and that is disposable once it has received a grade. The message of CityWorks, exemplified by the third goal, Producing High-Quality Work, is that there is a larger community of peers and adults who are interested in what they produce and that much of the work is indeed worth preserving. This goal becomes concrete for students through the process of designing and creating their own portfolio cases and binders.

An excellent way to introduce this activity is to bring in a professional who uses a portfolio as part of his or her work. An architect or graphic designer from the community or even a student teacher who has assembled a portfolio in preparation for getting a first job can show the students what a finished portfolio looks like, and in doing so reinforce the importance of high-quality work.

This is the first hands-on activity of CityWorks and hence the first time the teacher will have to deal with the management of materials and space that comes along with this type of work. For students to work productively on their portfolio cases and binders, they will need to sit at appropriate worktables or workstations where they can lay out the cardboard, and they will need to be responsible for their materials and tools.

Goal 4: Mathematics and Design

The activities and projects of CityWorks provide numerous contexts for students to practice their literacy, particularly writing and public speaking skills. Some projects also provide contexts for numeracy, learning to use relatively basic math principles to solve design problems. Students learn what it means to use mathematics in the design process (Goal 4) through designing a new tool. This involves learning how to use different scales for drawing objects and how to draw an object from different viewpoints. Math, art, and vocational teachers can all be helpful in introducing these concepts to students; the teacher may also want to bring in an architect or product designer to show the use of scale and viewpoint in the process of drawing out a design.

One of the advantages of bringing in an outside person is that the students have the opportunity to see how a professional makes a work presentation. This is something that the students themselves will be asked to do as the culmination of the tool design process. Although a number of earlier activities engage students in sharing their work, this will be the first more formal presentation to the whole group. It will be important to take time to go over the presentation tips (page 67) and to give students opportunities to prepare what they will say and how they will say it.

Goal 5: Problem-Solving

The ability to tackle semi-structured or unstructured problems is one of the "new basic skills" that students need to become productive adults. In City-Works, students have the opportunity to develop and practice that skill, beginning with the Technology Olympics and culminating in the community development project. In the Tech Olympics, students learn that some problems have many solutions, and that it is important to pay attention to key parameters in selecting one.

The Tech Olympics is also another opportunity to use mathematical concepts in envisioning solutions to design problems and to introduce the physical science concepts related to structural stability and forces. Students can design their vehicles without deep understanding of structural forces, but this is an opportunity to show them how to apply principles they may have learned in science classes. Again, depending on the teachers' own expertise, they may want to invite assistance from a physics teacher or a structural engineer.

Goal 6: Knowing the Community

The other major units of CityWorks focus primarily on community exploration and problem-solving. This theme is introduced through Goal 6, Knowing Your Community's Resources and Needs. Through a series of exercises focusing on landmarks, students practice seeing and describing the built environment and infrastructure of the community and envisioning what else could or should be there. Building on the skills they have been developing in the various design activities of this unit and their knowledge of their community, students construct three-dimensional models of landmarks—either ones that already exist or new ones that they think would add to the community. In creating the landmarks, students will reinforce their understanding of the design process, further hone their model-building skills, and begin to think about unmet needs in their community, which will form the basis of their work in later units.

WELCOME TO CITYWORKS!

In this course you will have an opportunity to learn about and make contributions to your community. At the same time, you will develop and practice important skills and personal qualities required for success in the world today. You will learn to work well in a team, frame and seek solutions to problems, communicate your findings to an audience, and hold yourself to high—and real-world—standards. You will also start to keep track of your own learning by writing entries in your own WorkLog and collecting samples of your work for a portfolio.

Introduction

The activities and projects of the next few months will help you understand each of the six goals of CityWorks. The first step is to look carefully at the list of goals. Then, your home team will start learning to communicate well (Goal 1) and to work together productively as a team (Goal 2) through games and activities such as writing biographies of each other. Because the work you do in this course is important, it should be done well and shared with other people (Goal 3). To make this possible, you will design and create a portfolio case in which to save what you have done. A number of the projects in CityWorks involve solving design problems, and this requires you to use mathematics. You will begin working toward Goal 4 by designing a new tool. By participating in a Technology Olympics you'll have the opportunity to practice both design and problem-solving (Goal 5). Finally, as a first step in knowing your community (Goal 6), you will focus your problem-solving and design skills on constructing models of landmarks in your community and begin to think about what your community has and needs.

Suggested Materials Box Contents

Each home team will receive a materials box with its own supplies. It is each home team member's responsibility to make sure that all supplies are well treated and returned to the box so that they remain available for the group's use. You should check to see that all of the team's supplies are in your box at the end of each class.

EACH MATERIALS BOX SHOULD CONTAIN

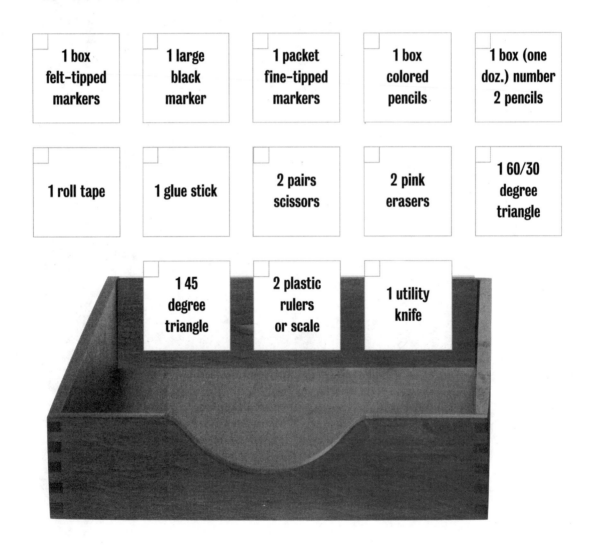

1 box felt-tipped markers	1 large black marker	1 packet fine-tipped markers	1 box colored pencils	1 box (one doz.) number 2 pencils
1 roll tape	1 glue stick	2 pairs scissors	2 pink erasers	1 60/30 degree triangle
	1 45 degree triangle	2 plastic rulers or scale	1 utility knife	

CITYWORKS GOALS

Working Well With Your Hands and Minds

Goal 1: Communicating Well

Being able to communicate ideas and information clearly—in written, oral, and visual forms—is an essential skill. In this "information era," it is especially important and challenging to gather, sort, and analyze information.

Goal 2: Working as a Team

In an effective team, members learn from one another and demonstrate mutual respect. By combining the skills and efforts of all of the members, a team can achieve higher levels of performance than could be accomplished by any single individual.

Goal 3: Producing High-Quality Work

Working carefully to produce high-quality results lets you take pride in what you have done. Keeping accurate portfolio records of the work you do allows others (a teacher, employer, or college admissions officer, for example) to see firsthand the skills you have developed and the learning processes you have gone through.

Goal 4: Using Math, Measurement, and Fundamentals of Design

Doing careful and accurate work in many career fields and industries requires an understanding of measurement systems, the ability to use mathematical reasoning skills, and familiarity with the fundamentals of the design process. Many ideas can be best understood and communicated through sketching and drawing and more precise modeling and graphic representation.

Goal 5: Using Problem-Solving Skills

In today's world we are often confronted by complex problems that do not have a single right answer. Rather, it is up to us to figure out how to approach the problem, test alternative ways of addressing it, evaluate these alternatives, and, finally, come up with a proposed solution.

Goal 6: Knowing the City's Resources and Needs

It is possible to live in a community for a long time without really being aware of what could improve the quality of life there or how to make necessary changes. An important first step is getting to know more about both the needs and resources of the community.

CITYWORKS GOAL 1
Communicating Well

Being able to communicate ideas and information clearly is important in all areas of life: at home, at school, at work, and in the community. CityWorks will give you opportunities to practice a variety of ways of communicating—through written, oral, and visual media.

Communicating effectively takes practice. Writing things down can help you express your opinions and organize your thoughts. The more you write, the better a writer you will become. A first draft is like thinking on paper. Through revising your work you can pay attention to making your ideas clear to other people. In CityWorks you will be asked to do several kinds of writing. You will keep a writing journal called a WorkLog to keep track of what you are working on in the class and record your thoughts about specific learning experiences. Your WorkLog will be read by the teacher, who will write comments back to you about what you have written. Try to write freely and in your own voice. At times, you will also write for a more public audience—summarizing what you have learned on Portfolio Record Forms, and writing brochures, newsletters, inter-views, or other finished pieces as final products for your project work.

Many people find speaking easier than writing. But oral communication is not as simple as saying whatever comes to mind. It certainly helps to listen attentively to the information or thoughts other people share with you. When speaking to colleagues, clients, teachers, or employers, it is valuable to know how to ask and answer questions. Looking at people when you speak to them also improves communication, by showing them that you are interested in what they are saying and allowing you to pick up signals from their body language about how they are feeling. Before getting up to make a presentation, it is important to gather your thoughts and make notes about what you will say.

TEAM EXERCISES

The Name Circle (This game is best when done with 6 or more players.)

Stand in a circle with your group. Have one member start by saying his/her first name, preceded by an adjective that both highlights one of his/her identifying character traits and starts with the same letter as his/her name, e.g., "perfect Paul," or "beaming Bini." The person to the right (or left) continues by repeating "beaming Bini" then adding his own name: "generous Gil." The third person repeats, "beaming Bini," "generous Gil," and adds "marvelous Marcus," and so on. As the game progresses around the circle, the list gets longer, and the task of repeating all of the names with adjectives will get more difficult. The last person must repeat every one's adjective and name and finish with his own. This is a fun and engaging activity to help the members of your group learn each other's first names as well as an identifying characteristic.

The Name Toss

Stand in a circle with your group and pass an item (anything easy to catch, from a ball to a rubber chicken) to each other as you say the name of the person you are tossing the item to. Once the item makes it to everyone in the circle, pass it around again and again while maintaining the original order of passing. To make this more difficult, another item can be introduced that must be thrown in the reverse order. Both items, plus an additional item, can be introduced at the same time once you and your group members get the hang of it.

CityWorks
Teammate Interview

This is good way to get to know the people in your home team. Complete the following exercises with someone in your group whom you do not already know. When you finish, you will introduce each other to the group. Write down or try to absorb as much as you can about what your partner is saying to use in your introduction.

What is your full name?

Where do you live?

What school did you attend last?

How long have you lived in the city?

Where else have you lived?
(Other neighborhoods, cities, countries)

When is your birthday?
(Do you know your astrological sign?)

What is your favorite music group or type of music?

What kinds of things do you like to do when you are not in school?

1. Take turns being the interviewer and asking your partner questions. You may use some or all of the questions listed below, but make up a number of questions of your own as well.

2. Talk to your partner and decide on at least two things you have in common with each other. This could be anything: where you live, the color of your hair, your favorite music (write down your responses).

3. Look at the map of the city and work with your partner to try to locate each of your streets and houses. Mark the location with a felt-tipped marker.

4. Now it's time for introductions. Begin by telling the group your partner's name and pointing out where they live on the map. Tell the group how your partner answered each of the questions and share any other information you learned about this person.

5. If there is time at the end of your introductions, have each person on the team draw a line on the map that shows how you get to the high school from your home. Use a colored pencil or marker to trace the streets you take to walk, drive, or travel by bus on your route to and from school. This will give the team a beginning sense of collective expertise about the community.

The Getting to Know You Game

You will have up to 20 minutes to see if you can find people in the room who fit the categories listed below and have them sign your sheet. The first person to complete a whole sheet wins a prize! You must follow these rules:

When you approach someone you must first introduce yourself, then ask them a complete question such as: Do you have an interesting hobby? Do not just ask: What things on this list can you check off?

You may only ask a person two questions, and have them ask you two questions before you must move onto another person, whether they have checked anything off or not. You can come back to the same person again.

When you approach someone who answers yes to one of the questions, complete the form by filling out their name and any other information required. Then have them put their initials next to the question.

No one may sign for more than four categories on your sheet.

1. Find someone who has gone swimming in the past two weeks.

Name _____
Initials _____

2. Find someone who speaks another language.

What? _____
Name _____
Initials _____

3. Find someone who hates pizza.

Name _____
Initials _____

4. Find someone who has an interesting hobby.

What? _____
Name _____
Initials _____

5. Find someone who plays a musical instrument.
What? _____
Name _____
Initials _____

6. Find someone who plans to be on a school sports team.

Which one? _____
Name _____
Initials _____

7. Find someone who has traveled outside of the United States.

Where? _____
Name _____
Initials _____

8. Find someone who has a pet.

What? _____
Name _____
Initials _____

9. Find someone who has a job.

Where? _____
Name _____
Initials _____

10. Find someone who has read a book in the past month.

Title? _____
Name _____
Initials _____

11. Find someone who is a middle child.

Name _____
Initials _____

12. Find someone who is the same astrological sign as you.

What sign? _____
Name _____
Initials _____

13. Find someone who has the same color eyes as you.

What color? _____
Name _____
Initials _____

14. Find someone who is within 1 inch of your height.

How tall? _____
Name _____
Initials _____

Partner Biography Project

When people become famous, authors write biographies of them. In this activity, everyone will have the chance to be profiled, and everyone will learn how to construct someone else's story. This activity allows students to go into more depth as they get to know another and also to build their writing skills.

Pick a partner. Each of you is going to interview and write a two- to three-page biography about the other. You will also be "presenting" your interview partner/subject to the class. Finally, you will evaluate your partner's written biography of you to determine if it is an accurate representation of who you are.

Note: This is a research project. Your research source materials will be primarily live interview subjects (people), but you will also attempt to gather written materials. If you were a professional journalist, biographer, or filmmaker, you would be using as many different source materials as possible.

To be done with your partner:

1. Create and write up a list of interview questions.

2. Interview your partner and take notes.

3. Interview other people (including adults) who know your partner.

4. Gather any written materials (e.g., articles, awards, stories, pictures, old report cards, birth records that your partner can provide you with or that you can locate on your own directly relating to the biography you are writing. Remember, the more proof you can get to verify things you are told, the more accurate your biography will be. Try to back up statements with as much documentation as possible.

To be done individually:

5. Sort through all for the information you have gathered. Organize your interview notes.

Write up a currently accurate biography on your interview partner. Be sure to document all information sources used in the written biography you produce. Include the proof! (See attached sheet.)

6. Introduce your interview partner to the class and present your biography.

To be done with your partner:

7. Write an assessment of the accuracy of your partner's biography of you. What should have been included that was left out? Was anything you said misinterpreted?

The final assessment of your project will take into account:

1. Your list of written interview questions

2. Your list of sources and source materials used

3. Your finished biography

4. Your presentation

5. Your assessment of your partner's work

Note: Each partner team must turn in their written work together, as a package, with assessments included.

Identity Chart

An "identity chart" is a chart or pictorial representation that tells:

How you identify yourself

What groups you identify with

How those groups identify themselves

How you think outsiders view you and your groups

Assignment:

Create an identity chart that includes

1. A picture of you at the center, with identifying information about your name, physical characteristics, and personality traits. This is you identifying yourself.

2. Comments from others about how they identify you. Do they think you are smart? Funny? Athletic? Attractive?

3. A list of least four groups you identify with. Examples of groups include: age/gender groups, football/baseball players, sports team groups, religious affiliations, socio-economic groups, racial/ethnic/cultural groups, occupational/job groups, hobby/interest groups, neighborhood groups.

4. Write-ups describing how you think outsiders view your identified groups.

Presentation:

You will be presenting your identity chart to your studio team.

Your chart can include: photographs and magazine photos; handwritten or type-written keywords, quotes, statements, or text; plus any other illustrations or materials you think are relevant to your identity.

Your text and images should be glued to the poster board provided. You can use rubber cement for any photographs you would like to have back.

The History of Your Name

Your name has a lot to do with how you view yourself, and how others view you. How you feel about your name, the images it calls to mind and the stereotypes associated with it, nicknames that grow out of it—all have an effect on your identity.

Assignment: Write a short essay on the history of your name, making sure you research and include information relating to at least the following three items:

1. Where the name came from

2. Who (if anyone) you are named after

3. What your name means

The CityWorks Resumé

Each of you already has a variety of different skills and experiences that you bring to the group. A "resumé" is a listing of all your interests, skills, and work experience to date. It is something that all employers look for when you apply for a job, and it should show you in your best light. In CityWorks you will be preparing a resumé that you may use to apply for work and internship opportunities. You will have the chance to add to it as the year goes on and you acquire new skills and experiences.

Think about all the things that you have done up until now to prepare you for the work world. Don't sell yourself short! There are a lot of things you already know how to do. These could include being bilingual (speaking more than one language), taking care of younger brothers or sisters, landscaping (mowing the lawn or gardening), doing secretarial work, or helping a relative to paint or build something. If you are having trouble coming up with ideas ask your teacher for help.

The resumé worksheet provided will help you assemble your information. It would also be a good idea to obtain some copies of resumés from adult relatives or school personnel so that your home team members can learn from them. Take a look at how the resumés are formatted and what kind of information they include.

When you have decided on a format and edited the text for your own resumé, use a computer to create your final version. Make sure to save the file so that you can add to and edit your resumé as you collect new skills and experiences during the year.

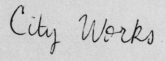

1. Your full name:

2. Address:

Note: In a formal resumé you would include your full address and telephone number.

For our purposes, however, a street name only and town will do.

No street numbers or phone numbers should be included.

3. Age, place, and date of birth:

4. Education level and school graduated from (years attended and graduated):

5. Any work experience, name of employer, and dates of employment:

6. Any special skills (include fluency — speaking and reading/writing — in languages other that English):

7. Hobbies, interests, and activities (include extracurricular activities, clubs, sports):

8. Awards and honors received (include honor roll, sports awards):

9. Educational goals and career interests:

RESUMÉ WORKSHEET

Personal Statement

Write a statement in which you describe your personal goals, ambitions, skills, and interests. Begin by taking time to think about what you would like to achieve in your life: as a student, as a worker, as a resident of your community, and as a citizen of the world. Reflect on the things that you enjoy doing and the skills that you have or would like to develop further. Think about your career goals and ambitions and how they relate to what you have done, or are doing now, in your life.

The goals you choose to write about may be short or long term, but they should give the reader a strong sense of who you are and what you value. An edited and typed copy of your Personal Statement will accompany your resumé as part of your CityWorks Portfolio. It will be the first item in your portfolio binder that people see and should paint an accurate and positive picture of who you are and aspire to be.

Communicating Well: WorkLog Reflection

Write a WorkLog entry describing the experience of writing your Personal Statement. You can use the ideas below to guide your writing or write about other things you have learned, discovered, and experienced.

Was it easy for you to write your Personal Statement? Why or why not?

Based on the short- or long-term goals you set for yourself in your Personal Statement, what do you think your statement says to people about who you are and what you value?

What decisions and choices do you think you will need to make within the next few years in order to move towards the goals you've set out for yourself in your Personal Statement?

NAME

DATE

THEME

PORTFOLIO RECORD

PARTNER BIOGRAPHY Attach a drawing or photograph of your partner.

Description of Drawing or Photograph

What was the process you went through to get the information you needed for your partner's biography?

What was it like to interview your partner? Did you get enough information during the first interview, or was it necessary to interview him/her more than once? What did you learn about the process of interviewing someone?

Note: you can use this form or the free-write Portfolio Record form.

Was it difficult to find source materials about your partner? What sources did you use?

Would you approach the project differently next time? Why or why not?

Which other partner biography projects do you think were done well? Why?

What did they reveal about the person?

Working as a Team

An efficient team works together to combine each person's skills to ensure good performance. In order to take advantage of the full potential of the team, it is important for everyone on the team to know as much as possible about what each member can contribute. Because some people are shy about sharing their strengths, CityWorks uses a series of group activities and games to begin the sharing process.

No matter how many skills are present in a group, the group will only function effectively if team members show one another mutual support and respect. This is most likely to happen if each person plays a role in setting the norms for acceptable behavior in the group and if everyone cooperates in creating shared work space. As part of forging your identity as a team you will have the opportunity to express what you need from other people in order to be an effective team member and to work together on creating a productive work environment.

One thing that really helps a group to coalesce is to address a challenging problem together. Several activities (such as the School Grounds Compass Course) will give you an opportunity to test out just how well your team has learned to work together. Before beginning these activities, take some time to discuss with your group members what each of you thinks are the most important elements of a good team.

HOME TEAM GROUP

INVENTORY FORM

Work with your home team to fill out the following.

We are a work team of (   ) members; (   ) are boys and (   ) are girls.

Our average age is (   ) . (   ) of us have grown up in _____

Other places some of us have lived include: _____

_____

We speak a total of (   ) languages, including:

If the school had a talent show, our "acts" would include:

The most unusual things we know how to do are:

(   ) of us currently hold jobs as:

Other jobs we have done in the past include:

(   ) of us regularly help out around the house by:

When we're not at school or at work, our main interests and hobbies are:

We know people who know a lot about:

Making Up the Rules

With your group, brainstorm a list of rules to help your team work well together. Write the rules on a piece of newsprint or on the blackboard. Once the team completes the brainstorm, have everyone look at the list in order to clarify any rules that are not clear and eliminate duplicates. Make a final list of rules and then discuss with your teammates examples of situations in which each rule would need to be enforced. These can be hypothetical examples or examples from each of your own experience. The point here is to ground the rule in some sort of context that everybody can relate to and understand.

Note: This list of rules should be written up neatly or entered into the computer in poster format. It will be posted on the walls to customize the home team space.

Choosing a Team Name and Creating a Logo

When choosing a name and creating a logo for your CityWorks home team, remember that your team name should represent your team in a positive way to the other members of the CityWorks class, as well as to the visiting professionals and community members with whom you will interact during the community development portion of the curriculum. It is helpful to keep in mind that the mission of the CityWorks class is to learn a combination of important academic, technical, and communications skills, while learning about the community, and performing a variety of projects that relate to the city's actual community development and community service needs.

Here are some words that might inspire you when you are talking about an appropriate name for your group. Add some of your own to the list before brainstorming about your group name.

Creativity   Action   Support   Quality Work   Teamwork   Success   Teen Visions

Once you have decided on a name for your home team, create a visual image that will serve as your team's logo identity. Your team logo can take many forms, such as a drawing, a symbol, or perhaps the name itself written in a particular font or writing style. Experiment with the graphic image and your name by drafting your ideas in pencil and markers, or by using a computer graphic software application such Illustrator or MacPaint.

You will be doing a final version of your logo and team name as part of the upcoming Home Team Work Space Project.

Home Team Work Space Project

In the CityWorks classroom, students and teachers share responsibility for keeping the CityWorks room clean and attractive. The CityWorks room has public spaces such as the presentation area and private spaces where the home teams meet. In this activity, each home team will work together for five to six class periods to fix up and customize their area.

Your group can fix up your space in many different ways, but you will be required to complete at least the following activities:

CREATE A TEAM LOGO (graphic identity and/or name), and then make a 14" x 14" laminated sign with your team name and logo on it.

Make a 17" x 22" laminated wall poster that lists the Team Ground Rules you created during the cooperative learning activity.

Clean tabletops and clean off all graffiti from wall and table surfaces.

Note: If possible, students might paint a wall, or walls, in their home team space.

STEP 1. BRAINSTORMING

Brainstorm with your group about all the ways you could make your home space a nicer and more efficient environment to work in. In addition to the required items listed above, you may also create artwork to go on the walls, bring in plants, create a "graffiti board," or bring in donated furniture.

STEP 2. CREATE A WORK PLAN

Your group cannot get started until completing a work plan approved by your teacher. Use the form provided to create your work plan which outlines:

- What you plan to accomplish as a group

- Who has responsibility for completing specific tasks

- Which tasks are top priority and should be completed first

- How long you plan to take for each task (for example: painting the wall will take 2 days for 2 people...)

STEP 3. GET TO WORK!

When working on your project, keep in mind the following rules:

- If your work space is used by other students at other times during the day, you will have to coordinate what you do with that group.

- You may not put graffiti directly onto walls or tables, but you can create a "graffiti sheet," which can be hung up in the room.

- You must allow enough time to clean up and put away paint brushes and other tools or materials you use during each period. Each group will receive their own set of painting tools, which they must take care of.

- Be sure to spread out drop cloths or newspapers when you paint. The floor and other room surfaces should remain free of paint!

Note: During this week you should bring in or wear older clothes and shoes to change into, clothes you don't mind getting dirty or paint stained. The paint that you will be using washes off with water, but it's better not to take the chance of staining good clothes. There also old shirts and aprons in the CityWorks storage room, which can be worn over your good clothes if you prefer.

WORK PLAN

1. Brainstorm with your group, then list each of your ideas for fixing up your area.

2. List those tasks that you will be performing as well as which person, or team of people, will be responsible for making sure that the task is done well and completed on time. Place your task list in order of priority by putting a number one beside the task that your group thinks is most important (using the space provided). Put a number two beside the next most important task, and so on. Finally, add the date you would like each project to be completed by.

Work Group

WORK
PLAN
WORKSHEET

Priority	Task List	Person(s) Responsible	Date to be Completed

List the materials you will need in order to complete your task list.

SCHOOL GROUNDS COMPASS COURSE

In this exercise you and your team will learn how to use a compass while working together to navigate your way through an orienteering course in the neighborhood near your school. Start outside at the main entrance to the school at the spot marked with an X. For the purpose of this exercise, 1 pace should be equal to 2' to 6". Record the path your team takes on the grounds map as you go along.

Note: These instructions and clues should be created by CityWorks teachers and include a scaled map of the school grounds. Examples of the compass course clues can be seen on the following page.

INSTRUCTION 1. Travel _____ paces at a bearing of _____ degrees.

Clue: _____

INSTRUCTION 2. Travel _____ paces at a bearing of _____ degrees.

Clue: _____

INSTRUCTION 3. Travel _____ paces at a bearing of _____ degrees.

Clue: _____

INSTRUCTION 4. Travel _____ paces at a bearing of _____ degrees.

Clue: _____

INSTRUCTION 5. Travel _____ paces at a bearing of _____ degrees.

Clue: _____

INSTRUCTION 6. Travel _____ paces at a bearing of _____ degrees.

Clue: _____

INSTRUCTION 7. Travel _____ paces at a bearing of _____ degrees.

Clue: _____

INSTRUCTION 8. Travel _____ paces at a bearing of _____ degrees.

Clue: _____

SAMPLE SCHOOL GROUNDS COMPASS COURSE

FROM THE RINDGE SCHOOL OF TECHNICAL ARTS

Start at the spot marked with an X outside the main entrance to the school. Record the path you are taking on your grounds map as you go along.

Note: The clues given in this example make reference in some way to attributes of each student destination point.

INSTRUCTION 1. Travel _____30_____ paces at a bearing of _____70_____ degrees.

Clue: *It's easy to get the hang of using a compass. Don't waste time spinning your wheels!*

INSTRUCTION 2. Travel _____56_____ paces at a bearing of _____125_____ degrees.

Clue: *Whatever happened to the old Cambridge Latin School?*

INSTRUCTION 3. Travel _____33_____ paces at a bearing of _____105_____ degrees.

Clue: *Step right down into the spotlight! Don't be shy; take center stage.*

INSTRUCTION 4. Travel _____92_____ paces at a bearing of _____South_____ degrees.

Clue: *What's the second largest country in North America?*

INSTRUCTION 5. Travel ___15/113___ paces at a bearing of _East/South_ degrees.

Clue: *The envelope, please... open your team's envelope.*

INSTRUCTION 6. Travel _____56_____ paces at a bearing of _____125_____ degrees.

Clue: *You're getting close!* ➤ 🍃

INSTRUCTION 7. Travel _____43_____ paces at a bearing of _____25_____ degrees.

Clue: *Give your sister a big hug!*

INSTRUCTION 8. Travel _____20_____ paces at a bearing of _____160_____ degrees.

Clue: *Life is a beach. Congratulations, you've made it!*

Basic Instructions for Using a Compass

How to take a bearing
(measure the angle between a landmark or object and magnetic north).

1. Hold compass flat and point direction of travel arrow toward the object or landmark.
2. Turn compass housing until orienting needle lines up with the magnetic needle.
3. Read bearing from compass housing circular scale at index line. Note: Close proximity to metal can cause the magnetic needle to register radically incorrect bearings.

How to measure a given angle from magnetic north in order to establish a direction of travel.

1. Set given bearing on compass housing circular scale at index line.
2. Hold compass flat and line orienting needle up with magnetic needle.
3. Travel in the direction arrow is pointing.
Note: It may help to choose a landmark while still holding the compass in line.
Reprinted with permission from Project Adventure, Inc.

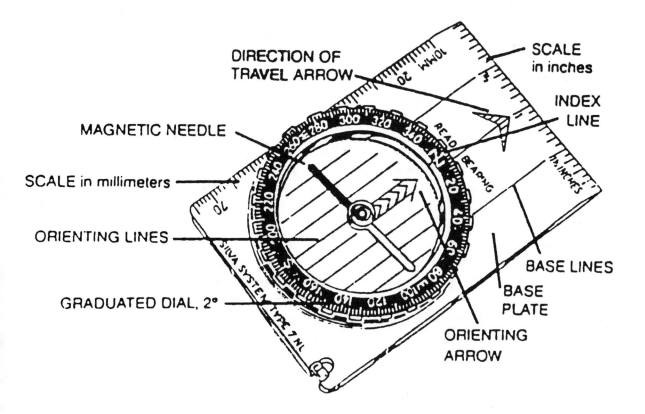

Toxic Waste Removal Exercise

Two circles of rope on the ground enclose highly poisonous zones, which cannot be entered or even reached across without serious injury. A #10 can stands in the middle of each zone. One is two-thirds full of highly toxic waste. It must be moved to the other circle and poured into the empty safe storage unit without spilling a drop. Safe removal equipment is provided: 6 10' ropes and 2 rubber loops.

Rules for the Removal, Transport, and Dumping of Toxic Waste

This exercise will be timed, for the purpose of seeing how quickly your team can work together to solve the problem. Five minutes of planning time will be provided before the timekeeping starts. Your team will have no more than 30 minutes to complete the task.

O No one may step or reach inside either toxic area, as defined by the rope loops on the ground.

O Only the materials provided (ropes and rubber loops) may come into contact with the toxic area.

O Neither the rubber rings nor the rope may touch the ground inside the circle. If they do, you will lose the ring, or a rope, depending on which one touched the ground.

O Toxic waste containers may touch the ground within either toxic area, but not outside a toxic area.

O Spillage within a toxic area means your team must start again from the beginning.

O Spillage outside a toxic area, or running out of time before completion will result in global environmental disaster!

"Toxic Waste Removal" is a good exercise for emphasizing group problem-solving, communication, concentration, teamwork, and leadership. After completing the exercise, talk with your group about the following: How did your group use your planning time? How did you allocate roles and tasks? How did the group respond to the time pressure? How did the solution come about? Whose ideas were used, under whose direction? How could you have done it faster?

Reprinted with permission from Project Adventure.

Developing Good Discussion Skills

This exercise will help your home team practice the skills
necessary for having a good group discussion.

Pre-Test

After choosing an interesting topic to discuss, or having the team
read a provocative article from the newspaper, carry on a
conversation with your team mates for a period of 5 minutes.
The team leader should circulate, listening, observing, and taking
notes on examples of good and bad discussion technique.
The section is called the "Pre-test."

After the Pre-test, hold a group discussion about what makes a
good discussion and what the barriers are. Next, you will practice
four skills necessary for good discussion. These skills are:
communicating clearly; listening actively; mirroring back; and
encouraging participation.

Communicating Clearly

Communication clearly involves getting quickly to the point.
Select a timekeeper who will watch the clock and keep time
for the group. Keep on discussing the subject for 5 minutes.
The timekeeper makes sure that each person talks for no more
than 20 seconds at one time.

Listening Actively

Listening actively means paying very close attention to what is
being said. Select a new timekeeper. Keep discussing the subject
for 5 more minutes, again making sure that each person talks
for only 20 seconds. This time, however, each person must wait
for at least 3 seconds after the person before has spoken before
he or she may speak.

Mirroring Back

Mirroring back is reflecting back to the group something essential about what the person before you has said. Select a new timekeeper. Keep on discussing the same subject, making sure that each person talks for only 15 seconds and that he or she waits three seconds after the other person has spoken before he or she speaks. In addition, everyone who speaks must begin by repeating to the group something that was said by the person who spoke immediately before.

This is called "mirroring back." The person who has just spoken must nod his or her head to indicate if he or she thinks this reflection is right. The new speaker may not continue until he or she correctly reflects what the person before has said.

Everyone Participates

All the people in the group have to speak. Select a new timekeeper. Keep on discussing the same subject for 5 more minutes. All previous rules apply, as well as a new one. No one may speak a second time until everyone in the group has spoken.

After each stage, ask each timekeeper to report on how well their group did on each skill being practiced. The timekeeper may have other observations to make about how difficult it was and what happened.

Post-Test

Select a person as observer who has not yet had a chance to play the role of timekeeper. Hold 5 more minutes of discussion without having to observe the rules but trying to use the four skills. Observers should note every example of a skill in use.

After the Post-test, ask observers to describe what they observed. Discuss some of the differences between the pre-test and the post-test.

Note: Have alternative discussion questions ready in case the group finishes with a discussion rapidly.

Developing Good Discussion Skills: Alligator River

Once there was a girl named Abigail who was in love with a boy named Gregory. Gregory had an unfortunate accident and broke his glasses. Abigail, being a true friend, volunteered to take them to be repaired. But the repair shop was across the river, and during a flash flood the bridge was washed away. Poor Gregory could see nothing without his glasses, so Abigail was desperate to get across the river to the repair shop. While she was standing, forlorn, on the bank of the river, clutching the broken glasses in her hand, a boy named Sinbad glided by in a rowboat.

Abigail asked Sinbad if he would take her across. He agreed, on the condition that while she was having the glasses repaired she would go to a nearby store and steal a transistor radio that he had been wanting. Abigail refused to do this and went to see a friend named Ivan who had a boat.

When Abigail told Ivan her problem, he said he was too busy to help out and didn't want to get involved. Abigail, feeling that she had no other choice, returned to Sinbad and told him she would agree to his plan.

When Abigail returned the repaired glasses to Gregory, she told him what she had had to do. Gregory was so mad at what she had done that he told her he never wanted to see her again.

Abigail, upset, turned to Darlene with her tale of woe. Darlene was so sorry for Abigail that she promised her she would get even with Gregory. They went to the school playground, where Gregory was playing ball, and Abigail watched happily while Darlene beat Gregory up and broke his new glasses.

Reprinted by permission of Warner Books, Value Clarification: A Practical Action-Directed Workbook by Dr. Sidney Simon. Copyright 1995.

Rank the characters from best (1) to worst (5).

Abigail   **Gregory**   **Sinbad**   **Ivan**   **Darlene**

Working as a Team: WorkLog Reflection

Write a WorkLog entry describing your experiences working as a team.
You can use the ideas below to guide your writing, or write about other things you have learned, discovered, and experienced.

How does learning more about the other people in your group make it easier (or more difficult) to work as a team?

What activities, sports, projects, or jobs are you involved in that require you to work as a team? Compare those teamwork experiences with the projects and exercises in this unit.

Do you think it will be important for you to develop good teamwork skills given the kind of work you imagine yourself doing as an adult? Why or why not?

NAME _____

DATE _____

THEME _____

PORTFOLIO RECORD

WORKING AS A TEAM
Attach a drawing or photograph of your team

Description of Drawing or Photograph

_____

_____

_____

Do you feel that your group began to work well together as a team? If so, during which exercise(s) or activity(ies) ? How and why do you think this happened?

_____

_____

What does your team do best together? For example, planning, allocating roles and tasks, meeting deadlines, communicating through work, communicating through discussion, problem-solving.

_____

_____

What is the process by which your team accomplishes these tasks or goals?

_____

What areas of teamwork should your group improve? What can your group do to improve these areas next time you work together?

_____

_____

Note: you can use this form or the free-write Portfolio Record form.

CITYWORKS GOAL 3
Producing High-Quality Work

By working carefully, persistently, and skillfully, everyone is capable of producing high-quality work. In CityWorks you will complete many different projects utilizing a variety of materials. Photographs, drawings, WorkLog entries, and the written records of all the work you do will be kept in a portfolio. Ultimately your portfolio will also include your personal statement, your resumé, a "record of accomplishment," and a table of contents to help you to organize your material.

You will now build a briefcase in which to keep your work. You may customize your portfolio briefcase in a number of ways so that it represents you and your work both personally and professionally. Your portfolio briefcase will contain folders in which you may store your project work. It will also contain a 3-ring "portfolio binder" in which you will organize examples of your work to showcase.

Save all of the written handouts (such as the record of accomplishment and goal sheets) that come as part of your portfolio information package inside your portfolio briefcase. You will need them at the end of each CityWorks unit, at which time you will assemble and update your portfolio materials.

About Your Portfolio

Your CityWorks portfolio will be a collection of your work displaying the important academic, technical, and communications skills you are learning. Your portfolio can also include work revealing the process by which you accomplished a particular project. You will be responsible for physically creating your portfolio briefcase, determining how it looks and what it says about you.

As more and more employers and colleges require applicants to show what they know and can do, it becomes important that you know how to develop a portfolio to showcase your abilities. You must demonstrate your mastery of your subject. For example, during a successful interview:

☞ A carpenter shows off finishing skills with photographs of finished cabinets.

☞ An information resource specialist demonstrates expertise through database samples and reports.

☞ A landscape designer brings sketches to show ideas.

☞ A day care worker provides lesson plans to show experience.

Your portfolio will help you to highlight your skills and experience. Working on your portfolio will help prepare you for your future. While developing your portfolio, you will have opportunities to collect work samples and to improve and practice both academic skills (such as writing and research) and technical skills (such as design and measurement).

Putting together a portfolio helps you see your own growth and achievements over time. Throughout the year you can review your portfolio and decide if you think you are doing the best you can do. This means that if you decide a section or piece needs more work, you can revise it! Finally, at the end of the year, the portfolio will be a record of what you have learned and how you have grown.

The first step in this process is to design and build a portfolio briefcase. The briefcase is where you will store and organize your work, in the form of drawings, photographs, writings, videos, or computer disks. On the following pages are examples of the forms you will use for collecting, categorizing, and sorting your work. After each CityWorks unit, you will take time to sort through work, do reflective writing, and add to your portfolios.

After constructing your portfolio briefcase, you will receive a portfolio binder, which you customize by creating a cover for it. The three-ring binder format will allow you to protect your work and reorganize it as necessary.

Designing and Building Your Portfolio Briefcase

Your CityWorks portfolio will consist of a portfolio briefcase constructed from a mat board, a three-ring binder, and various pocket folders for the purpose of storing and organizing your work. In this activity you will build and customize your portfolio briefcase.

Using the diagram shown as a guide, measure and layout the briefcase template on a piece of 20" x 32" colored mat board (this is exactly half the size of a standard size 32" x 40" board). All solid lines represent lines to be cut using a utility knife, while dotted lines should be lightly "scored" and folded. Scoring the surface of the mat board along the dotted lines insures that folded edges will be clean and crisp.

Additional directions for building your portfolio briefcase:

- Use a straight-edged ruler and a pencil to mark out the dimensions of your template on the mat board.

- Use a sharp utility knife to cut the mat board along solid lines, then lightly score and fold along dotted lines.

- Punch a hole in the front flap as shown.

- Use white glue or a hot glue gun to glue tabs. (A combination of both is ideal, as white glue will create a long-lasting bond, while a dab or two of hot glue will create an immediate bond that holds the pieces together while the white glue dries.)

- Insert canvas or nylon ribbon (approximately 1" wide x 11" long) through the slots, then glue on the inside ends, leaving enough slack for it to be used as a handle.

- Band all seams and edges with 1" colored masking tape if desired.

- Label the exterior of your portfolio case with your name and any other important information, then decorate or customize it as desired with computer-generated or freehand images.

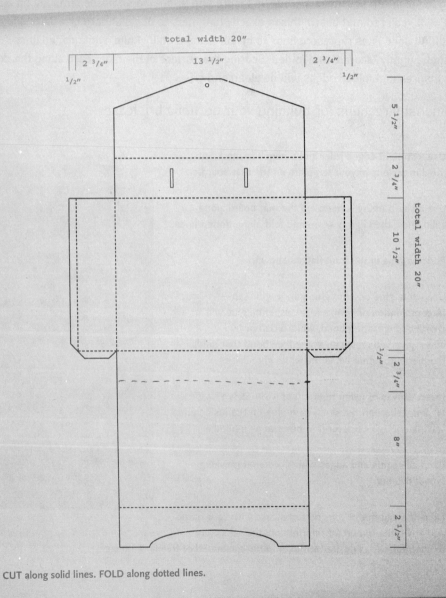

total width 20″

2 ³/₄″   13 ¹/₂″   2 ³/₄″

¹/₂″   ¹/₂″

5 ¹/₂″

2 ³/₄″

10 ¹/₂″   total width 20″

¹/₂″

2 ³/₄″

8″

2 ¹/₂″

CUT along solid lines. FOLD along dotted lines.

Customizing Your Portfolio Binder

Your portfolio binder is a three-ring binder in which you can store and organize the work samples you would like to showcase in your portfolio, as well as your personal statement, resumé, and record of accomplishment. Your portfolio binder will be stored in your portfolio briefcase along with other folders of your work.

You can personalize your portfolio binder by creating a portfolio binder cover and inserting it under the plastic view-binder. Your portfolio binder cover can include your name, your photograph, and some type of graphic image or drawing. Because the cover does so much to create a first impression, it is important that whatever design you create for it be executed to the best of your ability.

YOUR PHOTOGRAPH: Have a team member or your team leader take your photograph using a Polaroid or 35 millimeter camera.

YOUR NAME: Use a computer to generate your name or write/draw it out freehand. Try using different fonts to create the look you want.

A DRAWING OR GRAPHIC (OPTIONAL): This drawing or graphic should tell people something about who you are, what you like, and what you value. For instance, you could draw a sketch of your house, the logo for your favorite sports team or music group, a map of your neighborhood, or, if appropriate, the country that you or your parents are originally from. You could also use a graphic image that you like from a magazine, brochure, or book.

Putting Together Your Portfolio Binder Reference Sheet

At the end of each CityWorks unit, you will have the opportunity to organize your portfolio binder, catch up on work you are missing, update and/or improve the work samples you have, and decide what order to put your materials in. You will receive a set of forms to help you organize the contents of your portfolio. These should be kept in your portfolio binder for your reference throughout the year. Keep these reference sheets in your portfolio binder so that you have easy access to them whenever you need them.

Steps to Follow

1. Review CityWorks Goals 1 to 6 listed on Record of Accomplishment sheet.

2. Gather all portfolio material (refer to outline of projects provided at the end of each unit).

3. Update Personal Statement, Student Resumé, and Record of Accomplishment forms.

4. Select samples of work to illustrate achievement of CityWorks Goals. More than one sample may be included for each goal.

5. Prepare samples of work for inclusion in your portfolio by making sure that all work is clearly labeled, all writing pieces are edited, and other work samples are neatly presented. Samples can include: WorkLog entries, portfolio record forms, interview write-ups, captioned photographs, sketches, layouts, drawings, designs, video tapes, and computer discs. Note: If you know you created something during the year but don't have or can't find a record of it, you can make your own record by writing about it.

6. Fill in table of contents (do this only at the end of the year).

7. Punch holes in paper and insert in binder.

8. Complete cover for front of portfolio binder. Note: How your portfolio looks is important. You will want to make a good impression whenever you present your portfolio to an employer, an admissions officer, teachers, parents, or others. You may make a computer-generated or freehand drawing or illustration that can be inserted into the sleeve of your three-ring binder as a cover. This does not need to be the same as your briefcase cover.

Your Portfolio should demonstrate organization, neatness, accuracy and completeness.

Record of Accomplishment

In CityWorks, students develop a variety of important skills for life, work, and study. Below is a list of possible areas of student accomplishment based on the CityWorks learning goals. When organizing your portfolio binder, create cover pages for each of the six goals, and follow them with selected examples of your work which you think best address the particular goal.

1. Communicating Well
2. Working as a Team
3. Producing High-Quality Work
4. Using Math, Measurement, and Fundamentals of Design
5. Learning Problem-Solvling Skills
6. Knowing the City's Resources and Needs

Special Contributions (Extra time spent outside of class doing work on projects or presentations.)

Table of Contents

1. Student Resumé
2. Personal Statement
3. Record of Accomplishment
4. Learning Goal
5. Learning Goal
6. Learning Goal
7. Learning Goal
8. Learning Goal
9. Work Samples

What to Include in Your Portfolio

As you gather material for your portfolio binder and fill out your CityWorks Records of Accomplishment form, refer to the Putting it All Together for Your Portfolio sheets you receive at the end of each CityWorks unit. Look at the list of activities provided and think about the writing, planning, layout, and finished work you did for each of the projects you worked on.

You may include information from all phases of your projects, including initial planning, research and investigation, layout and production, and individual and group presentations.

You should also include the following items in your final portfolio:

- WorkLog forms
- Portfolio Record forms
- Drawings/Sketches
- Awards or Certificates (for good attendance, performance, etc.)
- Anything else you think is good example of your work that you would like to show others

About Your Portfolio Grade

Your CityWorks portfolio will receive a grade based on an assessment of its organization and presentation as well as how clearly it illustrates your mastery of each of the six CityWorks goals.

- Organization and Presentation of Portfolio
- Your portfolio should be organized so that people reading it can easily understand which items you have included and why
- Work is presented neatly
- Written work is typed or written legibly
- Written work has no grammatical or spelling errors
- Mastery of CityWorks Goals

Your portfolio should show that you have achieved a "competency level" for each of the CityWorks goals. This means that you have documented the process you went through for each of your CityWorks projects and included evidence of your learning such as: portfolio record forms, sketches, photographs, early drafts, and drawings.

Some teachers have used the following scale to grade CityWorks portfolios:

A = Achieved competency level on at least 5 goals

B = Achieved competency level on at least 4 goals

C = Achieved competency level on at least 3 goals

D = Achieved competency level on at least 2 goals

F = Did not achieve competency on any goals

PRODUCING

Write a WorkLog entry about high-quality work. You can use the topic listed below to guide your writing, or you can write about other things you have reflected on, learned, or discovered.

HIGH QUALITY

What do you think "high-quality work" means? Describe a piece of work or project you did that you think is high-quality. What about that piece of work makes it high-quality?

WORK: WORKLOG REFLECTION

NAME _____

DATE _____

THEME _____

PORTFOLIO MAKING   Attach a drawing or photograph of your portfolio case.

Description of Drawing or Photograph

_____

_____

_____

_____

_____

How did you go about creating your briefcase? Note the technical skills you needed to learn and use to design and build the portfolio briefcase.

_____

_____

_____

_____

What do you like and/or not like about the final briefcase product?

_____

_____

_____

_____

_____

Note: you can use this form or the free-write Portfolio Record form.

What did you do to make the cover of your portfolio binder reflect who you are, to convey your personality and sense of style?

How might you use your portfolio? What, if anything, is not clear about the purpose of your portfolio?

CITYWORKS GOAL 4

Using Math, Measurement, and the Fundamentals of Design

Math and design skills are used in many professions and industries. Having good basic math skills will help you do everything from simple measuring to putting together a budget or cost estimate to formulating and solving algebraic equations in real-life situations. Becoming familiar with the design process will assist you in conceptualizing and solving a wide variety of spatial and building problems. In this exercise you will learn a step-by-step design process to help you create a new tool, utensil, or product of your own design. This can be a modification of an existing tool/product, such as a spoon, toothbrush, or saw, or a new tool/product to address a new or unsolved problem. Before beginning your design drawings, it will be necessary to learn the basics about scaled drawings and drawing viewpoints.

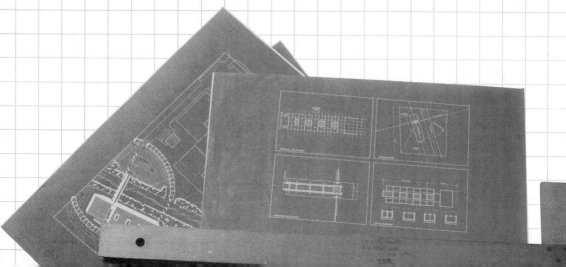

Object Scale

When drawing an object, such as the new tool/product design you will be creating, it is important to show it in its proper "scale." This means indicating the size of your design drawings or model in proportion to the actual size of the tool you are envisioning. Engineering and architectural drawings are small-scale representations of objects and buildings in which each of the component parts has been reduced proportionally to a specific scale.

Some commonly used scales for drawing objects are: 2" = 1", double scale; 1"= 1", actual scale; 1/2"= 1"; half scale, and 1/4"= 1", quarter scale. If we draw an object in the scale of 1/2" = 1" this means we reduce every inch, in real life, to 1/2 inch on our drawing. The scaled drawings of a matchbook below illustrate the use of these four different scales.

In order to practice using scale before designing your new tool, try drawing a variety of different hand-held objects and/or tools (for example, a hammer, scissors, or Walkman) in each of these four different scales. Use 1/4" graph paper for a scale reference, or draw your objects using a ruler or architectural scale.

Object Viewpoints

One of the first steps in designing and drawing a product or building is to learn how to show your design by drawing it from different viewpoints. In engineering and architectural drawing there are three primary views that help the designer to communicate her/his ideas: the Plan, the Section, and the Elevation.

The paper cup below shown below illustrates these three different drawing viewpoints for depicting objects.

PLAN
A view from above (as in a map)

SECTION
A flat cross-section (cut the cup in half: outline the contour)

ELEVATION
An upright picture of one side that is two-dimensional (flat)

Use 1/4" graph paper to practice drawing the three primary views of the objects you drew to scale in the previous exercise (the hammer, scissors, or Walkman).

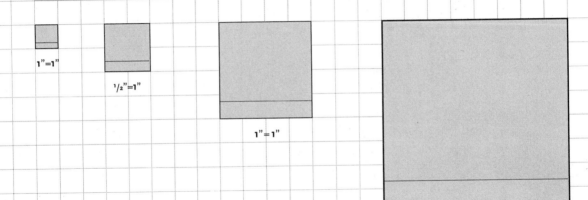

1"=1"

1/2"=1"

1"=1"

2"=1"

New Tool Design Project

Design is the process we use to shape the world and everything in it: products, packaging, clothing, buildings, landscapes, communication, transportation, cities—you name it! Design responds to people's changing needs, to new technologies, and to the environment. All designers go through a similar step-by-step problem-solving process as they create new design solutions. In this project you will be practicing this design process, working individually or in pairs to design either: a new kitchen utensil (i.e., spoon, fork, and/or knife) or any kind of new tool.

Design always starts with a problem to be solved or with something that needs to be created, invented, or improved. The problem-solving stages that must be followed in order to arrive at an effective design solution always involve a continuous feedback loop of design, evaluation, and redesign. One cycle of that loop can be outlined as follows:

1. THINKING/BRAINSTORMING **The designer must define the problem: what products already exist? How and why do they need to be modified or changed? What problems could be solved with a new design? What are all the possibilities for a new design? At this brainstorming stage, no idea is too crazy! In fact, crazy ideas could lead to some very creative solutions.**

2. SKETCHING/RECORDING **The designer uses sketches and drawings as if they were quick notes, to envision, develop, and evaluate new ideas. He/she also develops a list of design goals defining the problems to be solved.**

3. GETTING FEEDBACK **The designer shows his/her idea to clients and fellow designers** (in the form of drawings and simple models) in order to get feedback on whether or not the product is meeting the design goals.

4. EVALUATING **The designer evaluates the design in terms of what works and what doesn't work, taking feedback into account. He/she takes the best features from each design idea and combines them in order to create a solution that meets as many of the design goals as possible.**

5. PRODUCING **The designer makes an updated set of drawings and a model of the final product design.**

6. PRESENTING **The designer presents the final design drawings and model to the client.**

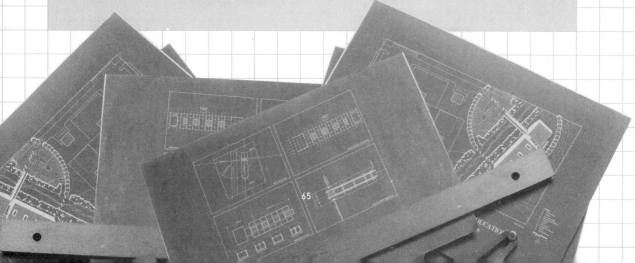

New Tool/Product Design Project

DAY 1: BRAINSTORMING

Think of an existing tool, utensil, or product that you would like to redesign or one that you would like to design from scratch. Ask yourself these key questions about the tool/product you have in mind and how it is used:

- ❏ Who uses the tool/product?
- ❏ Who doesn't, or can't, use it?
- ❏ What is the tool/product used for?
- ❏ How is it used? Why is it not used in other ways?
- ❏ Does it have multiple uses and purposes?
- ❏ How could you could change the way it is used?
- ❏ What materials is the tool/product made of and why?
- ❏ What are the key features of the tool/product? How is it designed and why?
- ❏ How is it different from similar tools/products?
- ❏ When is the tool/product used? Why not at other times?
- ❏ Is there a real need for this tool/product? What user needs are being met or not being met by it?

* This list of questions was adapted from a spoon design exercise developed by Rural Entrepreneurship in Active Learning (REAL).

Write the answers to these questions and any others you come up with, on a piece of lined paper. Think about the ways this tool could be modified or improved to work better, serve a different user group, or be modified for a whole new purpose.

DAYS 2 AND 3: SKETCHING/RECORDING

Draw sketches of your ideas on white paper or tracing paper. Draw your ideas with as much detail as possible. Try drawing the object from different viewpoints and angles. What does it look like from the top? The bottom? The sides? The inside? Refer to the Object Viewpoints student handout. You should also make decisions about how large your tool will be and what materials will be made from. On the third day you may begin to make a study model out of modeling clay or cardboard, if you think this would be helpful.

DAY 4: GETTING FEEDBACK

Present your ideas, your drawings, and possibly a study model made out of modeling clay or cardboard to the other students in your home team group. Get feedback from them about what seems to work well with your design and what might be modified.

DAYS 5 AND 6: EVALUATING/ PREPARING FINAL DESIGN AND PRESENTATION

Use the feedback you received from your team to make whatever modifications to your design necessary. Refine your design and prepare "final" colored drawings (use pencils or markers). Show a variety of views of your tool and label its important parts and features as well as the materials it is made of. Make a final "study" model out of modeling clay, cardboard, or whatever other materials seem appropriate. Finally, prepare a presentation in which you explain to your group about your design ideas for a new tool and show them your drawings and a study model. You will receive a handout with tips on how to make a good presentation as well as an outline you can fill out and use for your presentation.

DAY 7: MAKING YOUR PRESENTATION

Here's your chance to sell your design and tell people about all its wonderful features. This is like doing a TV commercial for your product—you must try to convince people they can't live without it!

New Tool Presentation Guidelines

At the end of the New Tool Design project, you will present your design to your class. Below is a list of the items you are responsible for completing within seven days.

A COLORED DRAWING, OR SERIES OF DRAWINGS SHOWING WHAT YOUR TOOL/PRODUCT LOOKS LIKE. You can draw it from the different viewpoints shown in your handout, and/or you can also show a "pictorial view" that shows what it would look like in three dimensions. Be careful to label all your drawings neatly with your name, the type of view you are showing, the scale you have used, and the important features and parts of your tool/product design. A section drawing, which shows a view of your tool/product as if you had cut it in half and could see inside, would be a good view to show.

A SCALE MODEL, WHICH SHOWS WHAT YOUR TOOL/PRODUCT WOULD LOOK LIKE, AND HOW IT WOULD WORK. You may use either cardboard or modeling clay to make your model. Think about which material would best suit your design. You should build your model at either full scale (life size), double scale (twice as big as in real life), or half scale (half as big as in real life). If your tool/products actual size is very large, you may have to use an even smaller scale for your model. The key to making a good scale model is to make sure that all the parts of your design remain "proportional" to each other.

TWO PRESENTATION OUTLINES, WHICH HIGHLIGHT THE POINTS YOU WANT TO MAKE ABOUT YOUR PRODUCT. Each presentation outline should be for a three-minute presentation. The first should be geared toward the board of directors of a bank who are deciding whether or not to give you money to finance your product. The second should be geared toward a group of your friends. You must write an outline for each of these presentations, although you will only be required to give one presentation to your home team.

Remember that your presentation is like a TV commercial for your design. You should talk about all of its best features including how it would work; why you designed it the way you did; what materials its made of; who would use it; how much it would cost; and why it's better than any other product on the market.

Presentation Tips

Good presentation skills are important, in school and in the workplace. Many people become nervous before making a presentation, but with practice they become better and better at it. Making a good presentation requires preparation. An outline can help you organize your thoughts and keep track of the main points you would like to make. Keep these tips in mind:

- ❏ Start by introducing yourself and your project.
- ❏ Speak loudly and clearly, so that your audience can hear you.
- ❏ Make key points that show a logical train of thought.
- ❏ Use an outline to help you remember your key points.
- ❏ Look at your audience and project your voice toward them.
- ❏ Don't stand in front of your project. If you block it, your audience won't be able to see it.
- ❏ Smile once in a while so that it looks like you are enjoying yourself.
- ❏ Show enthusiasm about your subject. You can't expect others to show interest in what you're saying if you don't!
- ❏ Finish by asking if there are any questions.

It also takes skill and practice to be a good audience member. Here are some points to remember:

- ❏ Do not talk (at all) when someone is making a presentation. Talking shows disrespect and makes it impossible for you and others to follow what they are saying.
- ❏ Look at the presenter and smile or nod your head once in a while to make it clear that you are paying attention and understand what he/she is saying. It's a lot easier for someone to make a presentation when s/he knows that the audience is "with them."
- ❏ Ask appropriate questions after the speaker has finished his/her presentation.

New Tool/Product Design: Presentation Outline

Your presentation can be geared towards a board of directors of a bank, or a television audience of teenagers. Outline a presentation including the following information:

- ❏ An introduction stating who you are and what your product is
- ❏ An explanation of how your product is used
- ❏ A description of all your product's special features
- ❏ A description of the different materials your product is made of
- ❏ An explanation of why your product is an improvement over other products like it, and why people should buy it (you could mention how much it would cost to buy)

NAME

DATE

NEW PRODUCT PRESENTATION OUTLINE

Glue photograph
or drawing of your tool/
product design here.

USING MATH,

■ Write a WorkLog entry describing your experiences using math, measurement, and the fundamentals of design. You can use the ideas below, or write about other things you have learned, discovered, and experienced.

MEASUREMENT,

■ Write about the ways in which you use math, measurement, and/or design in your everyday life (outside of school). Do you see a connection between the skills you learn in school and your outside activities? What kinds of math skills do you think are most important to learn in school?

AND THE FUNDAMENTALS

■ Are there things that you would like to do in the future that will require you to study more math and/or design? If so, what?

OF DESIGN:

■ Do you see your parents, or any other adults in your life using math or design skills in their work or in their life outside of work? How?

WORKLOG REFLECTION

NAME

DATE

PORTFOLIO
RECORD

NEW TOOL DESIGN PROJECT

Attach a drawing or photograph of your tool design or model

Description of Drawing or Photograph

Describe the process that you went through to create a design and a model for your new tool.

Were you happy with the way your project turned out? Why or why not? If you had it to do over again, what would you do differently?

Which was more difficult for you, drawing your design or making a model of it? Why?

Note: you can use this form or the free-write Portfolio Record form.

What projects designed by other students did you find most interesting? Why?

What do you think that you can learn from doing a presentation? What particular skills does doing a presentation help you to develop?

CITYWORKS GOAL 5
Using Problem-Solving Skills

The ability to think through and test out alternative solutions to a problem is important in school, at home, and in the workplace. By taking a step-by-step approach to looking at the various parts of a problem, you can imagine what the different solutions might be, then begin to test each one to see which works best. In CityWorks, many of the projects you will work on are like puzzles with more than one solution. Try to be open-minded about different ways to approach and solve each problem. The Technical (Tech) Olympics is an activity that will challenge you to use and further develop your skills in math, drawing, design, and building. In the Tech Olympics you will have the opportunity to work both individually and in teams to design and construct a variety of "vehicles" to safely transport an egg under treacherous conditions!

Technology Olympics: Suggested Training Activities

These training activities are designed as preparation for the Technology Olympics in order to help you further develop your abilities in drawing, design, paper/cardboard construction, and use of scale.

DAY 1: BASIC FORCES AND STRUCTURAL SYSTEMS

For this set of activities, consult with teachers from your school's math and/or science departments as well as with handouts on basic forces and structural systems from Mario Salvadori's book *Why Buildings Stand Up: The Strength of Architecture* (W. W. Norton, 1994).

Explanation of structural forces and demonstration of forces through group games (see Mario Salvadori books and videos)

Explanation of structural shapes and introduction of geometric patterns (see handouts on geometric shapes and patterns, pages 175-195)

DAY 2: CONSTRUCTING SHAPES AND STRUCTURAL ELEMENTS

Construct examples of at least three different structural shapes based on the Salvadori materials and three different geometric patterns based on CityWorks handouts for geometric shape patterns.

DAY 3: PAPER BUILDING EXPERIMENTS

Work individually or in pairs to build some kind of structure or object using all of the paper elements that you constructed (students are encouraged to assign a particular meaning or purpose to their creation, i.e., a building, or a car, etc.).

Do a sketch or drawing of your structure, object, or sculpture, labeled with your name and the name/title of your creation. You may shade and render your drawings if you have time.

DAY 4: PROBLEM-SOLVING

Brainstorm with your group the criteria for successful completion of the Paper Tower Project. This is a good way to see the relationship between defining the problem and creating standards for assessment. You may decide, for example, that the tower must be a minimum of 48" tall, must be aesthetically pleasing, and cannot be attached to the floor. When completed, the entries will be judged against these criteria. If the criteria are ambiguous or incomplete, you can talk about how to set clearer criteria for success on future CityWorks projects.

DAY 5: THE PAPER TOWER COMPETITION

Work with your home team to build a tower made out of newspaper, colored construction paper, and masking tape. Groups will have 15 minutes to brainstorm building strategies, then 30 minutes to build the towers. Towers will be judged by your fellow students based on the criterion decided upon by the whole group on day four. Constructive and destructive group process and teamwork skills should be observed and recorded by one studio member. After the activity, discuss these observations in a debriefing session. (See Paper Competition handout.)

Recognizing Geometric Shapes

Knowing how to recognize, draw, and construct a variety of geometric shapes will help you in the design of your Tech Olympics entry as well as any other types of building and design projects you do. Two-dimensional shapes are flat, while three-dimensional shapes appear to have depth. The ability to understand spatial relationships and work with shapes is essential in many professions. It allows you to design and create three-dimensional objects and helps you to read instructional diagrams, drawings, and blueprints. Complete the following exercises.

1. RECOGNIZING SHAPES

Write the name of all the two- and three-dimensional shapes drawn below in the space provided to the right of each shape.

2. DRAWING SHAPES

You can convert two-dimensional circles, squares, rectangles, and triangles into three-dimensional cylinders, cubes, rectangular solids, and pyramids. Use a blank piece of paper to practice drawing shapes in three dimensions by following the steps numbered below.

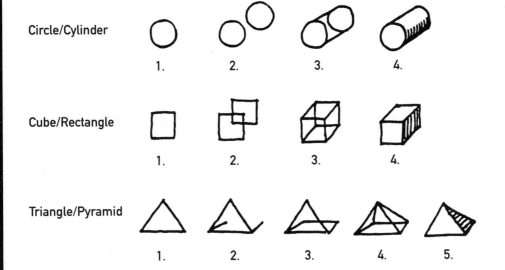

Circle/Cylinder
1. 2. 3. 4.

Cube/Rectangle
1. 2. 3. 4.

Triangle/Pyramid
1. 2. 3. 4. 5.

3. CONSTRUCTING SHAPES

Choose 6 out of the 8 different shape patterns supplied. Cut each shape out along the solid lines and fold them along the dotted lines in order to create three-dimensional shapes. Use rubber cement, tape, or glue to secure the tabs, creating a three-dimensional shape from your pattern.

Once your paper shapes have been constructed, combine them in new ways to create buildings, cars, sculptures, and so on. You can add detail to the shapes by using felt-tipped pens or colored pencils to add architectural elements such as windows, doors, and roofs. Try making your own patterns for new shapes that are either smaller or larger in scale or are new shapes altogether.

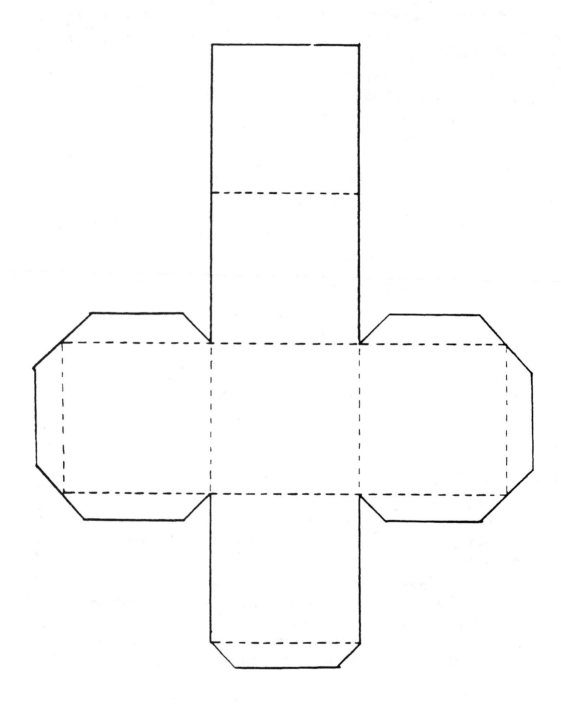

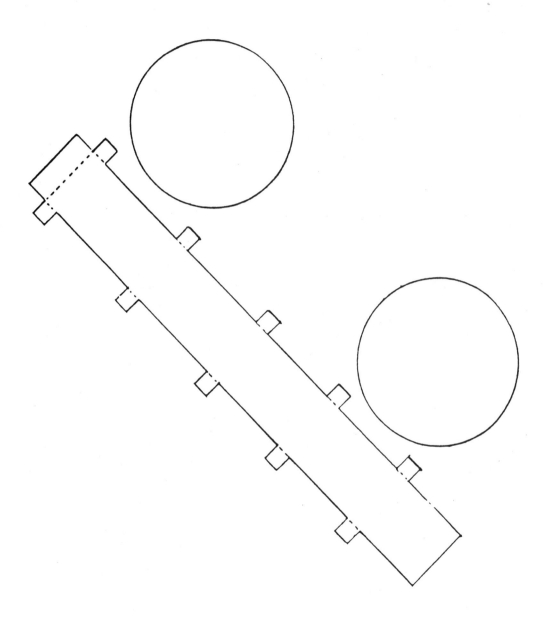

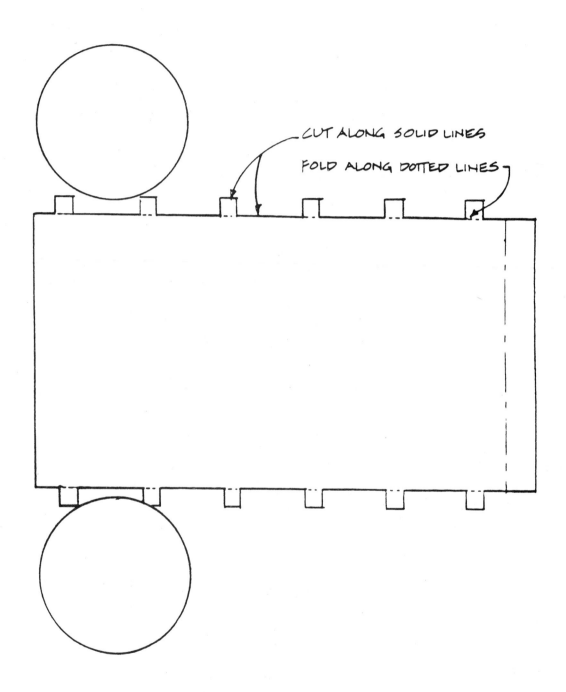

CUT ALONG SOLID LINES

FOLD ALONG DOTTED LINES

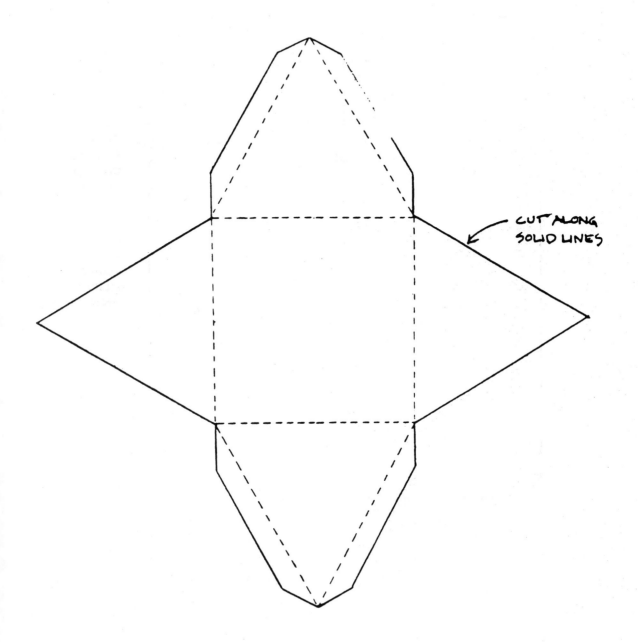

CUT ALONG SOLID LINES

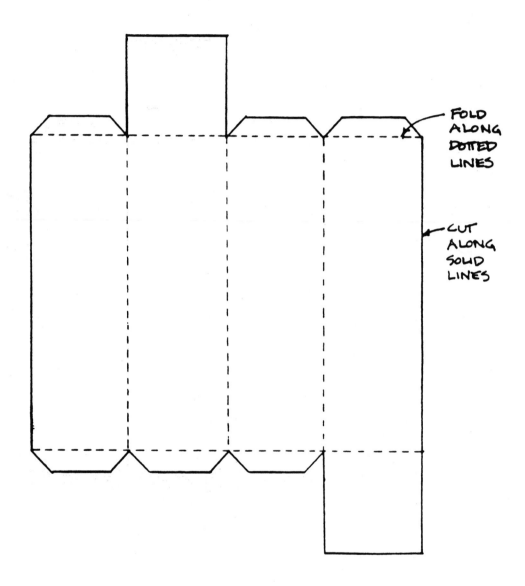

FOLD
ALONG
DOTTED
LINES

CUT
ALONG
SOLID
LINES

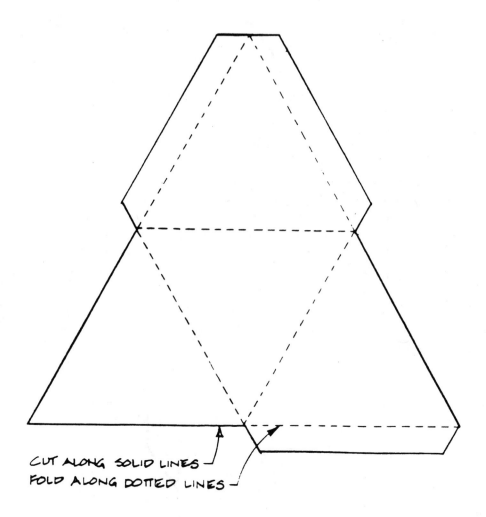

CUT ALONG SOLID LINES ⌐
FOLD ALONG DOTTED LINES ⌐

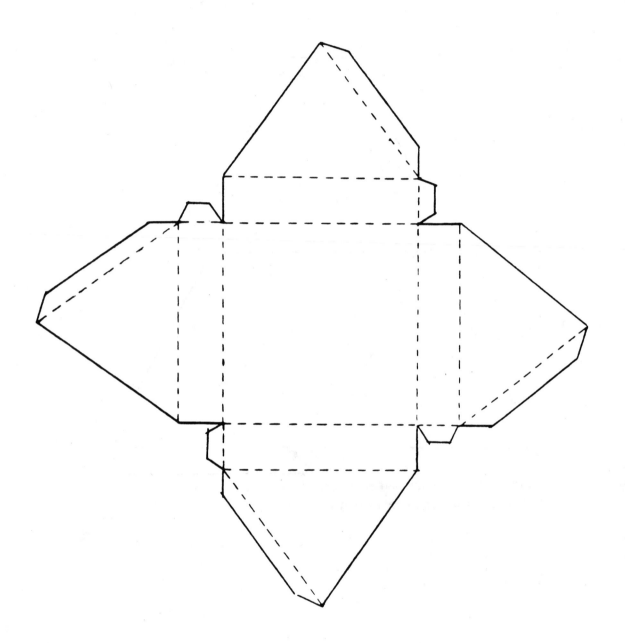

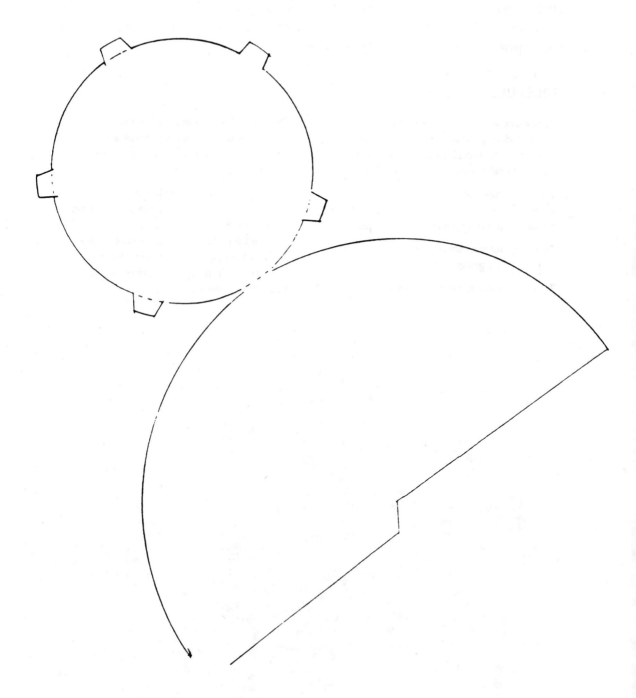

The Paper Tower Competition

In this activity you will have 45 minutes to work with your home team to build a tower made out of newspaper, colored construction paper, and masking tape. Your tower design must conform to the criteria for success developed by the larger group.

PROCEDURE

1. Assign one group member to act as an observer during the building process and to take notes about constructive and/or destructive group behaviors.

2. Take 5 minutes with your group to review the criterion for success decided upon by the larger group during the training activities.

3. Take 15 minutes to brainstorm building strategies with your group.

4. Take 25 minutes to build your tower.

5. Debrief with your group and group observer. Discuss how the building process went and what constructive and destructive behaviors people observed.

6. Present your tower to the larger group and have them vote on which tower(s) best meet the criteria for success. Discuss whether or not you think the criteria for success developed by the larger group were sufficiently detailed. In hindsight, what other criteria might have been set?

The Technology Olympics

In the Tech Olympics you will have the opportunity to work both individually and in teams to design and construct a variety of "vehicles" that will compete to safely transport a raw egg under treacherous conditions. There are five Tech Olympic entry categories listed below. For each category an individual or group decides to compete in, the participant(s) will be given a budget of three hundred "CityWorks dollars" with which to design, build, and test out an entry. Each student is required to submit at least one individual entry, while each studio group is responsible for at least one group entry. For those entries successfully completing the Tech Olympic competition by safely transporting the egg, there will be prizes for the fastest, lightest, most economical, and most ingenious vehicles.

TECH OLYMPICS ENTRY CATEGORIES

The Egg Drop

The Egg Crash

The Egg-o-Gram

The Wind-Powered Vehicle

The Air-Powered Vehicle

$10 CITY WORKS $10

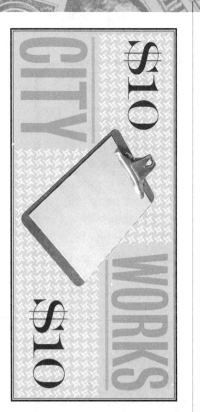

$5 CITY WORKS $5

$1 CITY WORKS $1

$100 CITY WORKS $100

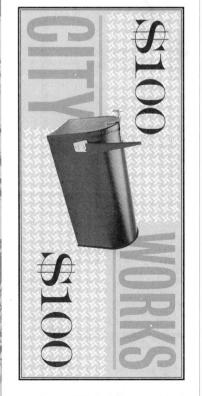

$50 CITY WORKS $50

$20 CITY WORKS $20

The Egg Drop

The goal of the Egg Drop exercise is to create a container for an egg which, when dropped onto concrete from a height of 20 feet, will protect the egg from breaking. You should use the problem-solving process to clarify your goals, create hypotheses, and test various design solutions before building your final Egg Drop container. Each Egg Drop entry must conform to the following guidelines.

COST: Studios will be given play money equal to $300 (CityWorks dollars) with which to buy materials to construct (and test) each of their Egg Drop entries. No entry may cost more than $300.

SIZE: Your container must be small enough to fit in a box which is 3 times x 3 times x 6 times the longest dimension of your egg. Note: anything used as part of your container design may have an overall diameter of no more than 4 times the longest dimension of your egg. Size regulations will be strictly enforced in determining prize eligibility.

You may use only the materials and tools listed below at the following costs:

Plastic straws	$15 each	**TOOLS**
White cardboard 11" x 17"	$50 per sheet	Glue Gun $20 per period rental fee (group rate) and $50 deposit
Rubber bands	$5 each	
White glue	$20 per period rental fee	Note: 4 pieces of 8 1/2" x 11" white paper will be provided to each student for making study models. White paper used for your final entry will be sold at $20 per sheet.
Masking tape	$10 per linear foot	
Glue sticks	$20 each	
Clear plastic	$50 per square foot	
White paper 8 1/2" x 11"	$20 per sheet	
String	$5 per linear foot	**All successful containers will be eligible for prizes.**
Wood skewers	$5 each	
Tongue depressors	$5 each	Winning categories:
Eggs	$5 per day egg leasing fee with $30 deposit (nonreturnable if broken)	1. The Most Economical
		2. The Best Design
		3. The Lightest

NAME

DATE

TEACHER

THE EGG DROP: MATERIAL COSTS & DRAWING

Make a list of the materials you will need. Consider costs and amounts carefully. Remember to figure in costs for rental of the glue gun and white glue, as well as the leasing of your egg.

Material and Tools (list below)	Cost
Total Cost:	

Drawing

Make one or more drawings or sketches of ideas for your Egg Drop container. Try drawing your container from various viewpoints (e.g., from up above and from the side). Label its significant features.

The Egg Crash

The goal of the Egg Crash exercise is to design and build a vehicle capable of transporting a raw egg down a steeply inclined racetrack and into a brick wall without the egg breaking. You will be given a limited amount of materials with which to build your vehicle, so plan your design carefully before you buy, and use your materials! Each studio will be given $300 (CityWorks dollars) with which to buy materials, rent tools, and lease eggs. No entry may cost more than $300 to build.

Materials available are:

White cardboard 11" x 17"	$50 per sheet	White glue	$20 per period rental fee and $50 deposit
White paper 8-1/2" x 11"	$20 per sheet	Masking tape	$10 per linear foot
Rubber bands	$5 each	Glue sticks	$20 each
Metal washers	$20 each	Clear plastic	$50 per square foot
String	$5 per linear foot	Eggs	$5 per day egg leasing fee with $30 deposit (nonreturnable if broken)
Wood skewers	$5 each		
Tongue depressors	$5 each	**TOOLS**	
Paper clips	$1 each	Glue gun	$40 per period rental fee (group rate)
Plastic straws	$15 each		

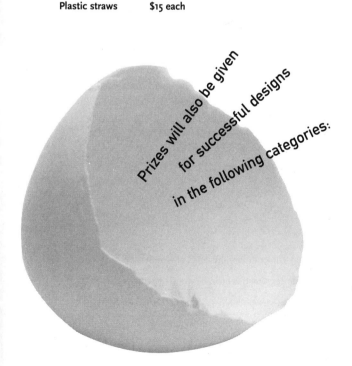

Prizes will also be given for successful designs in the following categories:

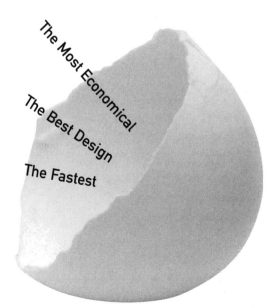

The Most Economical

The Best Design

The Fastest

NAME

DATE

TEACHER

THE EGG CRASH
MATERIAL COSTS
& DRAWING

Make a list of the materials you will need. Consider costs and amounts carefully. Remember to figure in costs for rental of the glue gun and white glue, as well as the leasing of your egg.

Material and Tools (list below)	Cost
Total Cost:	

Drawing

Make one or more drawings or sketches of ideas for your Egg Crash vehicle Try drawing your vehicle from various viewpoints (e.g., from up above and from the side). Label its significant features.

The Wind-Powered Vehicle

The goal of this exercise is to create a very fast wind-powered vehicle from a limited number of materials and have it travel farther than any other contestant's wind-powered vehicle.

COST: Each studio will be given $300 (CityWorks dollars) with which to buy materials to construct and test each of their wind-powered vehicle entries. No entry may cost more than $300.

SIZE: Your vehicles may not exceed 14 inches in any direction.

MATERIALS: You may use only the available materials and tools at the following costs:

Plastic straws	$15 each	String	$5 per linear foot
1/32" White cardboard	$50 per square foot	Wood skewers	$5 each
White glue	$20 per period rental fee	Tongue depressors	$5 each
Masking tape	$10 per linear foot		
Glue sticks	$20 each	TOOLS	
Clear plastic	$50 per square foot	Glue gun	$20 per period rental fee (group rate) and $50 deposit
8 1/2" x 11" white paper	$20 per sheet		

GUIDELINES

1. You may work alone or with a partner.

2. The vehicle should demonstrate a sense of craftsmanship.

3. Your name and studio group logo must be clearly shown on your entry.

TIPS

1. Quickly sketch some ideas before you settle on one design.

2. After you think through any problems, build a miniature prototype out of paper.

BUILD YOUR VEHICLE!

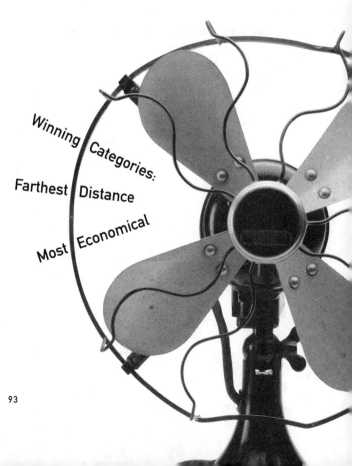

Winning Categories:
Farthest Distance
Most Economical

NAME

DATE

TEACHER

THE WIND- POWERED VEHICLE MATERIAL COSTS & DRAWING

Make a list of the materials you will need. Consider costs and amounts carefully. Remember to figure in costs for rental of the glue gun and white glue, as well as the leasing of your egg.

Material and Tools (list below)	Cost
Total Cost:	

Drawing

Make one or more drawings or sketches of ideas for your Wind-Powered Vehicle. Try drawing your vehicle from various viewpoints (e.g., from up above and from the side). Label its significant features.

The Egg-o-Gram

Packaging designers use a great deal of imagination in developing containers to protect their contents. Damaged goods are costly to manufacturers and retailers. Some elaborate packaging often costs more than its contents.

THE PROBLEM

1. Design a package which will contain one or more empty, whole chicken eggshells of medium size. To remove the yolk and egg white, pierce the egg shell with a large needle or pin, and then blow the contents out through the pin hole.

2. The package must protect its contents when delivered to the school via the mail.

3. The package may not bear "fragile" or any other wording indicating a need for special handling.

4. The volume of the package may not exceed 100 cubic inches per eggshell shipped. Therefore, three empty eggshells may be mailed in a package with a maximum volume of 300 cubic inches.

THE LIMITATIONS

1. A maximum of $1.00 (U.S. currency—not CityWorks dollars) may be spent on materials used to build your Egg-o-Gram. If you did not actually purchase the materials you are using, you must estimate their cost based on retail prices.

2. The package must be mailed third class.

NAME

DATE

TEACHER

THE EGG-O-GRAM
MATERIAL COSTS
& DRAWING

Make a list of the materials you will need. Consider costs and amounts carefully. Remember to figure in costs for rental of the glue gun and white glue, as well as the leasing of your egg.

Material and Tools (list below)	Cost
Total Cost:	
Weight of Egg-o-Gram:	
Cost of Mailing:	

Drawing

Make one or more drawings, diagrams, or sketches of ideas for your Egg-o-Gram. Try drawing your package from various viewpoints (e.g., from up above, from the side, or in section to show how it is constructed). Label its significant features.

TECH OLYMPICS
MATERIAL REQUEST FORM

NAME

DATE

TEACHER

Budget:

Materials and Tools:	Cost:	
Total cost of materials and tools:		
Amount left in budget before purchase:		
Amount left in budget after purchase:		

USING

- Write a WorkLog entry describing your experiences using problem-solving skills to design and build your Technology Olympic vehicle(s). You can use the ideas below to guide your writing, or write about other things you have learned, discovered, and experienced.

PROBLEM-SOLVING

- Based on your experience in the Technology Olympics, what do you think are the most important steps and skills necessary for designing and building?

SKILLS:

- Do you feel that the design decisions you made were good ones? Would you approach the problem differently next time? If so, how?

WORKLOG REFLECTION

- What do you think are your strengths and weaknesses in problem-solving? Describe times in your life you have had to solve a problem.

NAME

DATE

PORTFOLIO RECORD

THE TECHNOLOGY OLYMPICS

Which category(ies) of vehicle(s) did you work on developing and building for the Technology Olympics?

Did you work with a partner to design and build an entry? If so, what is the experience like? Did you work well together? Why or why not?

Glue photograph or drawing of your tech olympics entry here.

Note: you can use this form or the free-write Portfolio Record form.

How did you go about the process of designing and building your vehicle(s)?

Would you do it differently next time? Explain why or why not.

What did you learn from using the CityWorks money system, which required you to plan and budget

for the materials you used to design and build your vehicle?

Did your vehicle's performance in the Technology Olympics competition surprise you in any way?

Why or why not?

Knowing Your Community's Resources and Needs

As students and future (or present) workers, it is important that you learn about the resources and needs of the community in which you live. What can the community/city offer you? What can you offer the community? In this series of exercises you will have the opportunity to look at the existing resources, services, and landmarks in your community and think about new resources, services, and buildings you would like to create. Using the technical skills you practiced during the Tech Olympic activity, you will then design and build models of existing landmarks as well as new "fantasy" landmarks for the community.

The City Quiz

See how much you know, or can guess, about the neighborhoods, industries and ethnic groups in your city. Later you will be brainstorming about what new landmarks, buildings, and services you would like to see in the city.

1. In what year was the city first settled, and what was its original name?

2. How many people live in the city?

3. What percentage of the city's inhabitants are school-age children? What percentage of voters have children of school age?

4. Is the city racially, ethnically, and socioeconomically diverse? What percentage of the city's residents are white (non-Hispanic)? Black? Hispanic? Asian? Other races?

5. List four of the nationalities represented by people who live in the city.

6. List the names of four neighborhoods in the city.

7. What are some of the nicknames for neighborhoods in the city? List two.

8. Who is the top employer in the city?

9. List four industries located in the city.

10. Which industry employs the most people?

11. How is the city governed?

12. What is the median income of people who live in the city?

13. Name a famous person who grew up or lived in your city.

What's a Landmark?

A landmark can be many things: a prominent and identifying feature of a natural landscape; a building or place that has historical significance; the site of an event marking a turning point in history; a fixed marker that everybody knows about; or a popular building or service in the community. The city has many landmarks. Your job right now is to identify which of those landmarks are most important to the city, and then choose one to recreate as a scaled architectural model. You could also choose to design and build a model of a new "fantasy" landmark, which would provide new resources to the community.

To help you reflect on the community's existing landmarks and resources, look through this list of categories into which many of them fall, and think about specific examples.

Parks and recreation

Historical sites

Schools

Universities

Public transportation buildings or areas

Housing complexes

Businesses and retail stores

Malls and shopping centers

Institutional and municipal buildings

Corporations

Hospitals

COMMUNITY LANDMARKS WORKSHEET

Take some time to brainstorm with your group about the different landmarks in your community. Then list those you think are most important. Next, list those landmarks you think are most popular with, or important to, teenagers. Record your top five choices for important community and teen landmarks below.

Community Landmarks

1.

2.

3.

4.

5.

Teen Landmarks

1.

2.

3.

4.

5.

Now think of what kinds of buildings, services, and landmarks don't currently exist in the city but would be great to have. These can be your "fantasy landmarks." For example, you could create a giant sports stadium, a teen dance club, or a lake for swimming in the summer and skating in the winter. List your fantasy landmarks below.

Fantasy Landmarks

1.

2.

3.

4.

5.

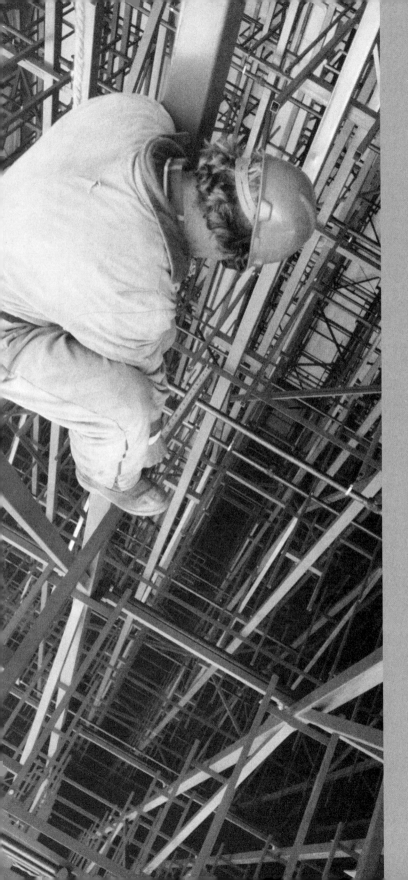

Building a Landmark

In this exercise you will use three-dimensional shapes to build a model of a landmark. Select one of your community, teen, or fantasy landmarks. Which would be the most interesting to build out of construction paper? Think of a model that would use at least two or more of the shapes you've learned to build. You may need to invent shapes of your own or combinations of shapes.

Your first step will be to lay out the patterns on construction paper for the shapes you will need for your model. You can make the model as small or large as you like, although it should be in an appropriate scale so as not to become too difficult or material-intensive to build. Once you decide on a building scale, make sure all of your proportions are consistent. When you have laid out the patterns you can draw windows, doors, or any other details using markers, pencils, or pens.

After finishing your model you will be locating it on a large map of the city drawn on the floor. If you have created a fantasy landmark, think about where in the city it would be best located and why.

Four Things to Think About When Designing and Building Your Landmark

1. SCALE

Model scale is like map scale. It is a system of measurement that allows you to reduce the size of what you are designing, drawing, or building so that it is represented as a fraction of its actual size. As with your tool design project, you will be using scale to help you build your landmark model so that it is accurate in detail and proportion. Once you decide on an appropriate scale for your model, use 1/4" graph paper or an architectural scale to help you lay out your patterns.

2. SHAPES

It will be necessary for you to identify the shapes you will need to build your new or existing landmarks. You will be using 1/32" cardboard and construction paper to build your model, and you can refer to the shape pattern handouts for clues about how to draw the patterns you will need. You may be required to combine shapes and patterns in order to create three-dimensional shapes that are unusual and/or specific to your building.

3. VIEWS

Think about how your landmark looks in plan, elevation, and section view (see Drawing Views handout). Your elevation views will tell you a lot about what the various side walls of your model will look like.

4. DETAILS

Think about the important details and architectural features your landmark has, and be sure to draw or build them to the correct scale. If you are building an existing landmark, and it is a building, find pictures or make sketches to record important details such as types of windows, doors, columns, and roof slopes. If you are designing a new landmark, think about what details would be most important to show.

Drawing Scale

When drawing a building or an object it is important to show it in its proper "scale." Scale is the size of a representation in proportion to the size of what it represents. Architectural drawings are small-scaled representations of a building with each of its component parts reduced proportionally to a specific scale. Design drawings of objects also use scale to indicate relative size and proportion. When drawing your design for a new tool you will need to choose an appropriate scale for your drawing.

The most commonly used scales for drawing buildings are 1/8", 1/4", and 1/2". When we draw in one-eighth-inch scale (1/8") that means that we reduce every foot (1'), in real life to one eighth of an inch on our drawing. We label this scale on our drawing by saying the 1/8" = 1'-0". One-quarter-inch scale means that every foot is reduced to 1/4", and half-inch scale means that every foot is reduced to 1/2". The drawing of a six-foot-tall person below illustrates the use of these three different scales.

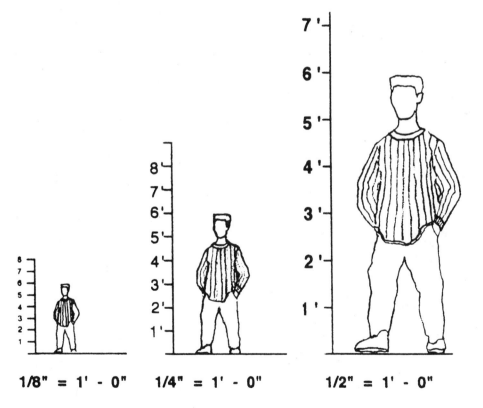

1/8" = 1' - 0"   **1/4" = 1' - 0"**   **1/2" = 1' - 0"**

Drawing Viewpoints

One of the first steps in designing and drawing a building or a product is to learn how to show your design by drawing it from different viewpoints. In architectural drawing there are three primary views that help designers communicate their ideas: the Plan, the Section, and the Elevation.

Here are some drawings of a building which show the same three views.

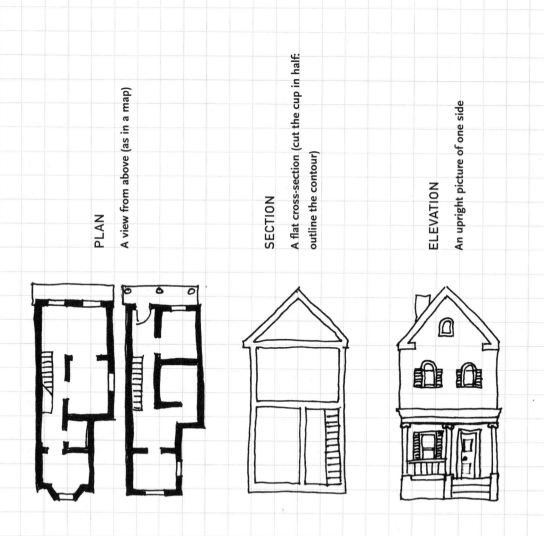

PLAN
A view from above (as in a map)

SECTION
A flat cross-section (cut the cup in half, outline the contour)

ELEVATION
An upright picture of one side

Presenting Your Landmark

You will each present your landmark to your class. If you have built a model of an existing landmark, see if your fellow students can guess what it is. If they are having trouble, give them some clues about what significance the landmark holds for the community. Talk about the process you went through to build your model and any challenges you faced.

If you made a design and a model for a new community landmark, see if your classmates can guess what it is. Be prepared to talk about where you plan to locate the landmark in the city and why. Share with the group why you decided the community needed the particular new landmark, building, or service you created.

After everyone has presented his/her landmarks, put them all out on display and have class members vote on winners for the categories listed below.

COMMUNITY LANDMARKS: VOTING SHEET

NAME

Write in the name of the landmark you think should win for the categories listed below.

Existing landmarks:

Existing landmark most important to the community:

Most realistic model of existing landmark:

New landmarks:

New landmark that best meets the needs of the community:

Most interesting new building design:

Landmark that has most potential to become a successful business:

KNOWING

- Write a WorkLog entry describing the community in terms of its resources and needs. You can use the ideas below to guide your writing, or write about other things you have learned, discovered, and experienced.

THE COMMUNITY'S

- Which resources in your community do you think are most plentiful or deficient? Why do you think this is so?

RESOURCES AND NEEDS:

- What have you learned about the community's resources and/or needs as a result of doing Landmarks?

WORKLOG REFLECTION

- What new businesses, services, or resources does the community need most and why?

- Where might someone who has just moved to the community go to find out what resources were available to him/her?

NAME

DATE

LANDMARKS PROJECT
Attach a drawing
or photograph
of your landmark

Name and location of landmark

Why did you choose to make this landmark? How is the landmark important to your city?

If it is a fantasy landmark, how would it be important to your city?

List all of the different geometric shapes and patterns you used to make your landmark.

Describe the process of making your landmark. Where did you get the idea? How did you lay out the shape

patterns? How did you detail or decorate your building?

The Individual and the Community: Putting It All Together

Now that you have finished the CityWorks unit entitled The Individual and the Community, it is time to review the projects you have completed thus far, individually or as part of your home team, and begin to assemble records of your work to be organized within your portfolio binder. These records can take the form of WorkLog reflections, Portfolio Record forms, photographs of projects, work samples, interviews, drawings, videotapes, computer disks (with stored project work)—anything that will communicate to others who you are, what you have done in CityWorks, how you have done it, how you feel about it, and what you learned in the process.

Make sure that all of the written work included in your portfolio binder is edited. Both written and visual work should be well labeled and neatly presented. Below is a list of project work you should have completed during the past few months. If you need to write any missing Work-Log reflections or Portfolio Record forms, if you would like to update or edit those you have already completed, or if you need to put the finishing touches on any project work you plan to include in your portfolio binder as a work sample, take the time to do it now.

As you go through each of your products, review the six CityWorks goals listed on the Record of Accomplishment form you received as part of your packet of portfolio materials (see page 20). Although each CityWorks activity corresponds to a particular CityWorks goal, (in terms of how the curriculum is organized), you will find that many of your products could be used as examples of a number of these goals. Once you have made a cover sheet for each goal and put it in your portfolio binder, you may organize your work samples in whatever way you think makes most sense.

The Individual and the Community Project List

Partner Biography

Identity Chart

The History of Your Name

CityWorks Resumé

Personal Statement

Communicating Well: WorkLog Reflection

Partner Biography: Portfolio Record Form

Making Up the Rules

Choosing a Team Name

Home Team Work Space Project

Working as a Team: WorkLog Reflection

Working as a Team: Portfolio Record Form

Designing and Building Your Portfolio Briefcase

Creating and Customizing Your Portfolio Binder

Producing High-quality Work: WorkLog Reflection

Portfolio Making: Portfolio Record Form

Object Scale and Object Viewpoints

New Tool Design Project

New Tool Design Presentation

Using Math, Measurement, and Fundamentals of Design: WorkLog Reflection

New Tool Design: Portfolio Record Form

Drawing and Building Three-Dimensional Shapes

The Paper Tower Competition

The Technology Olympics

Using Problem-solving Skills: WorkLog reflection

The Technology Olympics: Portfolio Record Form

What is a Landmark?

Building a Landmark

Presenting Your Landmark

Knowing Your Community's Resources and Needs: WorkLog Reflection

Landmarks Project: Portfolio Record Form

UNIT 2

WalkAbout the Community

- INTRODUCTION for the Teacher
- INTRODUCTION for the Student
- WalkAbout the Community
- Putting it All Together for Your CityWorks Portfolio

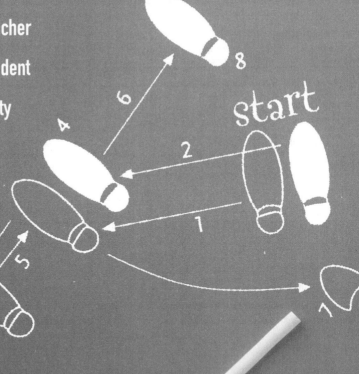

INTRODUCTION FOR THE TEACHER

The WalkAbout Unit serves as an apprenticeship in project design and management and specifically in field-based investigation. Students select different aspects of life in the community to explore through observations, interviews, and other forms of research. The exercises and activities in this unit are designed to support them through this process and teach them the skills they will need. (See Notes to the Teacher, page 14, for a discussion of how to support students in project-based learning).

One of the most important aspects of an apprenticeship is the opportunity to develop skills within a context where the culminating performance or final product and the standards of excellence are clear. Under the tutelage of the master, apprentices perform tasks through which they develop the skills that will enable them to attempt their own first master-work.

Students know from the beginning of the WalkAbout that they will engage in a field investigation and will present their findings both visually (in a presentation board format) and orally to an audience of peers, teachers, and community members. Knowing that this is the ultimate goal, they can make choices about whom to interview, where to visit, and what other forms of research to do. They will also understand why it is important for them to learn the skills involved in doing interviews, taking photographs, making maps, and assembling materials in a strong visual format on a board. The more they understand the context of what they are doing, the more likely that they can begin to make their own assignments, hence bringing to the work a greater sense of purpose and focus.

WalkAbout the Community begins with several short activities to help to focus students on the process of neighborhood investigation and to build the skills they will need to carry out this type of study. First, students prepare "report cards" on neighborhoods in the city that they know. The exercise helps them to think about what makes a neighborhood a good place to live. Then students do several exercises that introduce them to map-making, specifically to creating easily recognizable symbols for their maps. Each student applies these skills to create a walking tour and a map of his/her own neighborhood. The collection of individual tour maps from each home team becomes a group presentation board, a good "dry run" for the final presentation board required at the conclusion of the WalkAbout.

The culminating activity of this unit is for each home team to select a study area (a five-block radius) near the school and a focus theme that guides them in an investigation of this area. For example, one home team may choose to focus on arts and culture, while another investigates health issues. Whatever the theme, the team conducts interviews with residents about this theme and visits particular institutions or agencies within their study area that relate to this theme (e.g., the arts and culture group might look at public art in their area). They may choose to venture outside of the study area to visit an important community institution relating to their theme (e.g. the health group may decide to visit the city hospital to interview someone there about services available to local residents).

Ultimately, the quality of the work students do will depend on their personal investment. In a project like the WalkAbout, where the broad parameters are set by the teacher, it is especially important that students have a say in the particular focus theme their group investigates. This is why the unit begins with each group of students filling out a focus theme application, citing their top choices, and then writing a proposal explaining why they would like to do fieldwork related to that particular theme. The teacher can choose to view the proposals competitively, selecting the best one for each theme and then giving the other students their second choice, or allow several groups to investigate the same theme, perhaps in different neighborhoods. The important thing is that each group of students feels invested in their work.

WALKABOUT THE COMMUNITY
Introduction

You and your home team will spend the next few weeks working on a study of the city's neighborhoods called WalkAbout the Community. Your task will be to act as detectives, collecting observations, information, and clues about what goes on in particular neighborhoods and areas of the city. First you will look at the neighborhood you live in, creating a tour and a map so you can teach others about its important characteristics. Then your home team will choose a "study" area near the school for your group to investigate in more depth.

What's a Neighborhood?

Most cities are divided into areas called neighborhoods that have particular boundaries (edges) and characteristics. There are "official neighborhoods" or zones defined by the city government. There are also many unofficial or "personal neighborhoods" defined by the residents of the city.

All neighborhoods have different features, such as: types of houses and apartment buildings, stores, parks or playgrounds, schools, community buildings, and hangouts. Through the WalkAbout, you and your team will investigate the neighborhoods surrounding the school and look at what kinds of resources they provide to residents of the city.

The members of your home team probably already have a lot of collective knowledge about the city's various neighborhoods. Do these exercises together and see what your group can come up with.

Do the following exercises using the map of the city provided:

1. Find your street and the approximate location of your house on the map. Think about the boundaries of what you think of as your "personal neighborhood" or turf. Are the boundaries formed by streets and buildings, or are they imaginary boundaries? Do you think that other people in your neighborhood acknowledge the same boundaries? Use a colored pen or pencil to outline what you think are the boundaries of your neighborhood. The outlined area should include at least your residence or dwelling, your street, friends' houses, and nearby parks or stores that you use.

2. Brainstorm with your group to make a list of the city's "official" and "personal" neighborhoods. Using different colored pencils or markers, outline the boundaries of, then label, each neighborhood you can think of.

3. Brainstorm, then list some of the nicknames used for neighborhoods in the city.

Grading Your Neighborhood

In order to get a clear picture of the city's neighborhoods and what they have to offer, it will be important for each home team to put together as much information as possible about the good points and the bad points of the city's neighborhoods. In this exercise, think about your own neighborhood or another neighborhood you know well and grade its features, using the report card on the back of this sheet. Add any other features you think are important for a neighborhood to have.

When your home team members have each filled out their neighborhood report cards, discuss them with each other. Do you all have similar ideas about what constitutes a good or bad neighborhood? What features on the report card do you think are most important and why? Do you think that people's ideas about what they value in their neighborhoods change as they get older? What other features did you add to your report card lists and why?

NAME

DATE

NEIGHBORHOOD NAME

What makes a neighborhood a good place to live?
Grade your neighborhood on the following features, then add
other features you consider important and grade those.
Refer to the grading chart below. Give reasons for your grade.

NEIGHBORHOOD REPORT CARD

Housing: Are houses and apartment buildings clean, safe, and in good repair? GRADE:

Public Transportation: How accessible is the neighborhood by bus or subway? GRADE:

Stores: Are there food stores with good quality and selection of foods at affordable prices? GRADE:
Are there clothing stores with good quality and selection of clothes at affordable prices?

Schools: Are there schools within walking distance? Are they considered good schools? GRADE:

Grading Chart: A = Definitely yes   B = Yes, with some reservations   C = Maybe   D = Not really   F = Not at all

Recreational Facilities: Are there playgrounds, fields, basketball/tennis courts, other sports facilities?   GRADE:

Is there an indoor gym that residents have access to?

Open Space and Parks: Are there trees, yards, public spaces in which to walk and sit?   GRADE:

Parking: Is there enough parking for people's cars? Is there off-street parking?   GRADE:

Noise: Is it peaceful and quiet, relatively undisturbed by traffic or street noise?   GRADE:

Safety: Is the neighborhood safe to walk around in, even after dark?   GRADE:

Other: GRADE:

Other: GRADE:

Other: GRADE:

Grading Chart: A = Definitely yes   B = Yes, with some reservations   C = Maybe   D = Not really   F = Not at all

Symbols

Symbols are images that have meaning. They can be pictures, drawings, shapes, letters, or numbers. Symbols are like a language. Anyone can use or read a symbol once they know what the symbol stands for.

Symbols usually show pictures or letters to give you clues about what they represent. The symbols on this page are ones that you may already know. See how many you can identify by labeling each symbol in the space provided. If you're not sure what the symbol represents, take a guess!

1

2

3

4

5

6

7

8

9

10

11

12

Individual Mapping Symbols

Symbols can be used on maps to represent things one finds on a street, such as sidewalks, buildings, stop lights, trees, and mailboxes. You and the other members of your home team will each create symbols to represent the physical features of your community. As preparation for an exercise in mapping your neighborhood, take some time to make up symbols for the items listed below and draw them in the boxes provided. Remember that symbols usually show pictures to give you clues about what they represent.

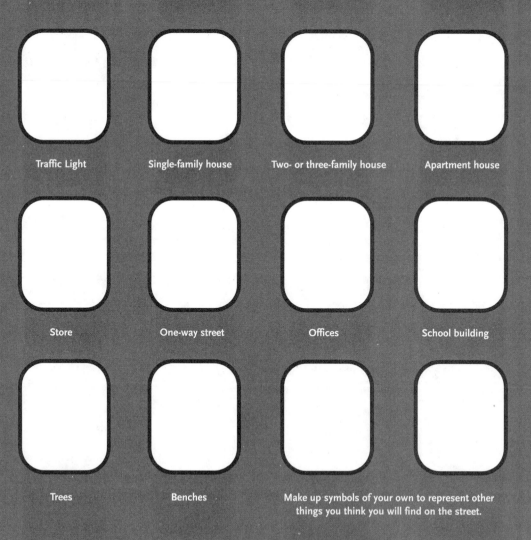

| Traffic Light | Single-family house | Two- or three-family house | Apartment house |

| Store | One-way street | Offices | School building |

| Trees | Benches | Make up symbols of your own to represent other things you think you will find on the street. |

Group Mapping Symbols

Choose some of your favorite individual mapping symbols you created and share them with your home team. Decide among your group which symbols to adopt as your "group" symbols. Which symbols are the clearest, simplest, and easiest to understand? You may want to take a vote on which symbols to adopt for each item or decide to combine elements from a few different symbols. Once you decide on your group symbol for each item, draw them in the boxes below, making sure that everyone in your home team is drawing the symbol in the same manner. Save this sheet as reference for the neighborhood mapping exercise.

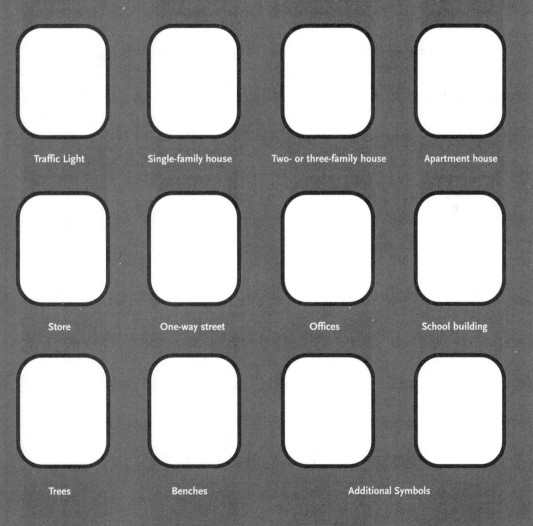

| Traffic Light | Single-family house | Two- or three-family house | Apartment house |

| Store | One-way street | Offices | School building |

| Trees | Benches | Additional Symbols | |

Tour Your Neighborhood

In order to get a complete picture of the city it will be necessary to pool all of our knowledge about each of the city's neighborhoods. The neighborhood you know the best may be the one that you live in. If you were giving someone a tour of your neighborhood, how would you describe it to them? Think about the kinds of people who live there as well as any other special characteristics you think are important. Also think about the places and/or buildings that are an important part of your neighborhood. Answer the questions below and then proceed to the mapping exercise.

Name and Location of Neighborhood:

Characteristics of Neighborhood:

Five Important Places or Buildings:

Map Your Neighborhood

Use the space on this page to draft a rough map of the neighborhood you live in. Then use your own paper to produce a finished version. Your map does not need to be drawn perfectly, but it should be as detailed and accurate as possible. Show your street, your residence or dwelling, and any other buildings or places you listed on your neighborhood tour sheet. Make your drawing clear and easy to read. Use the mapping symbols you created with your home team to represent the buildings and objects on your neighborhood map, labeling its buildings, streets, and significant features.

Group Neighborhood Presentation Board

After each student in your home team has gathered information about his/her neighborhood, put together a group presentation board that contains each student's neighborhood tour map as well as a location map of the city. Highlight your neighborhoods on the location map and present your own map and neighborhood tour sheets to the other members of your home team.

■ Write a WorkLog entry about the neighborhoods in your community. You can use the ideas below to guide your writing, or write about other things you have learned, discovered, and experienced.

NEIGHBOR-

■ How would you describe the variety of neighborhoods in your community? Are they very different from each another? What sets them apart or gives them their particular identity?

HOODS

■ After completing the Group Neighborhood Presentation Board exercise, are there any neighborhoods or areas in the community you would now like to visit or explore further? What specifically interested you about those neighborhoods?

WORKLOG REFLECTION

■ Why do you think people sometimes create conflict over neighborhood "turf," or feel a need to "protect" their neighborhood? Describe a personal situation involving neighborhood loyalties and/or conflicts.

Investigating a Focus Theme

In the WalkAbout the Community activity, your home team will spend the next few weeks investigating a "study area" through the lens of one of 16 different community "focus themes." This project requires you to research and record information. Skills you will use include: taking photographs, interviewing, drawing site plans, sketching pictures, and building models.

After your group has done all its explorations you will put together presentation boards to display the information gathered and illustrate conclusions reached. At a minimum, your group must include the following types of information on its presentation boards:

• A summary of your focus theme and its importance to the city

• Photographs that provide important visual information about your focus theme, the people you spoke with, and the sites you saw

• Typed interviews with people who have ideas and opinions about (or experience with) your focus theme

• Drawings to illustrate some aspect of your focus theme

• A plan and symbol legend showing the location of the study area in relation to the school as well as important buildings or features of the area pertaining to the focus theme

In order to have a variety of topics covered, every group will be encouraged to focus on a different theme or a different aspect of the same theme. Your group must fill out a "Focus Theme Application," which lists your first three choices, along with a "proposal" for what kind of information the group plans to obtain for each theme and how you plan to get it. You're most likely to get your first choice if you make a strong, clear proposal about what you plan to do.

In addition to choosing a focus theme, your group will also decide on a study area that lends itself to being examined through the lens of the theme you have chosen. The area should be approximately five blocks in size and be easily accessible from the school. The area may be residential, commercial, industrial, or a mixture of all three. This will be your team's "study area" for the remainder of the WalkAbout the Community activity.

Choosing Your Focus Theme

Look at the list of WalkAbout Cambridge "focus themes" below and decide with your home team which themes you might like to investigate. List your choices from one to three, then create a "proposal" for your first and second choices. Remember that whether or not your home team is awarded the focus theme of their choice is based on how many other groups apply for the same theme and how complete and viable your proposal is. Your proposal should detail the following information:

- What you would like to find out about the focus theme

- What your questions are about your focus theme

- How you would go about doing your investigation

- Whom you might interview in order to get information

- Where your group might go in order to gather information

- What field trips outside of your study area may be necessary

- What study area or areas you think would lend themselves well to being examined through the lens of your proposed focus theme

Focus Themes

Arts and Culture

Communications

Community Issues

Education

Employment

Entertainment

Health

History

Housing

Immigration

Ownership and Control

Parks and Recreation

People and Demographics

Quality of Life

Retail and Business

Transportation

Zoning

After your home team has received approval on a focus theme, (hears about which of your focus theme choices you will get the opportunity to pursue) you will be asked to submit a final proposal with a more detailed plan of action.

Focus Theme Ideas

Remember that you and your team can investigate your focus theme in many different ways, using observations, photographs, interviews and written records. Each group will put together boards to present its findings. Your boards can include things such as drawings and sketches, bar and pie graphs, three-dimensional models, and two-dimensional boards. It's up to your group to decide which features of your focus theme to highlight. Here are some ideas; see if you can add to them.

Focus Theme: Arts and Culture

What kinds of cultural events (fine art, music, movies, dance, drama) are available to people who live and work in the area?

Is there any public art in the area? Who was the artist who created it and how did he/she get the commission? Is public art important to a community? Why or why not? Where would be a good place to put a public art project in the area?

Are there any museums or other cultural centers in the area? If so, what is the history of the building? Is it an integral part of the neighborhood?

What new business or services with artistic or cultural value could be started in the area?

Other ideas?

FOCUS THEME: **Communications**

What kinds of media outlets exist in the area?

How do the people who live and work in the area get their information about what is happening in the city and in the world?

What new communications businesses or services could be started in the area?

How has modern communication technology affected the personal lives and work lives of the people who live and work in the area?

Is the study area near the school? If so, how do people in the neighborhood communicate with the school community? Could the school improve its communication with the outside world? Would it want to? Why or why not?

Other ideas?

FOCUS THEME: **Community Issues**

Interview people in the area to find out what they think are the most important issues affecting them and the community.

Interview people at the city hall, the Office of Community Development, or the city's Police Department to find out what they think are important community issues affecting the area.

Talk to residents about issues of crime and safety in the neighborhood.

Interview residents or businesses about the local economy and how it affects them.

Think of ideas for new services or buildings which could be created in the area.

Other ideas?

FOCUS THEME: **Education**

What educational institutions are available to the people who live and work in the area?

What kinds of jobs do the people who work for these educational institutions have?

What other services and benefits are provided to the area by educational institutions?

What is the history of particular educational buildings or institutions in the area?

Other ideas?

FOCUS THEME: Employment

Record all the different kinds of jobs that exist in the area, including those generated by home or building owners who improve their property.

Profile a business in the area. Who owns it? How long has it been there? Interview the owner and the people who work there. How has the local economy affected them?

Profile someone who works in the area. Interview them about their employment history. Take his or her photograph and write up the interview.

Find out about the different kind of jobs or businesses that may have existed at one time but are no longer there.

Describe the kinds of new jobs or businesses that could be created in the area.

Other ideas?

FOCUS THEME: Entertainment

Interview people in the area to see what their favorite forms of entertainment are.

What entertainment options exist in the immediate area for children? For teens? For adults?

What new forms of entertainment or recreation would people like to see in the area? Where could they be located?

Profile a person who lives or works in the area who is in the entertainment field.

What did people in the area do fifty years ago for entertainment? Twenty years ago? How is that different from what people do now?

Other ideas?

FOCUS THEME: Health

What kinds of health care facilities are located in, or accessible to, people who live and work in the area? Are people aware of these facilities?

What concerns do people who live and work in the area have about health care in the city in general?

What kinds of health care "packages" are available to workers? The elderly? The unemployed? What options do people have who do not have health care?

Are people health-conscious in this area? Interview people in the area to see if they think they eat well and if they exercise regularly.

Other ideas?

FOCUS THEME: History

How has the area changed over the past 100 years? Interview older people to see what they can tell you.

Visit the city's historical society and find pictures of and information about the history of the area in terms of its residents and buildings.

Copy old pictures of the area and take new pictures to show how the street has changed.

Find out which are the oldest and newest buildings in the area.

Think of new ways in which you would like to see the area develop or change.

Other ideas?

FOCUS THEME: Housing

What kind of housing exists in the city? Who built it? Who lives there? How does someone go about finding a place to live? Make a pie or bar graph showing different housing types.

How old are the different types of houses and apartments? What styles of architecture are they? Visit the local Historical Society.

Where has new housing been built recently? Who developed the property and who will live there? Who can afford to live in the city and who can't? What kinds of new housing does the city need?

What are the major materials and construction techniques used for housing in the city? Have they changed over the years?

What are some of the most common architectural details on houses and apartment buildings in the city? Do drawings of the buildings or details you see on the buildings. Record the colors of the houses.

How much does it cost to rent, or buy, different types of houses in the city? How different were prices two years ago? Ten years ago? Thirty years ago? Do a cost analysis of a building that includes the cost of purchasing and renovating a home in your neighborhood.

Other ideas?

FOCUS THEME: Immigration

How has the ethnic profile of the people who live and work in the area changed over the past ten years? Thirty years?

What ethnic groups are represented in the neighborhood? Are there a number of distinct ethnic groups that can be identified? If so, what are their distinguishing characteristics? How do the various ethnic groups in the area relate to each other?

Interview and profile a child, teenager, or adult who lives or works in the area and who immigrated from a different country. How has his/her life changed since immigrating? What was his/her immigration experience like? Write an oral history or make a video about his/her story.

What services does the city offer to its immigrant population? What new services could be created to better serve immigrants?

Other ideas?

FOCUS THEME: Ownership and Control

Go to city hall or interview people in the neighborhood to find out who owns what buildings or houses and for how long.

Do a profile of a building or buildings in terms of who has owned the building, when ownership changed hands, and how the value of the building has changed.

Discuss issues of home or business ownership. Investigate how to apply for mortgages, who gets them and how eligibility is determined.

Other ideas?

FOCUS THEME: Parks and Recreation

What kinds of green space are accessible to people who live and work in the area?

What do teenagers who live in the area do for recreation? Where do they go?

What new recreational activities, businesses or services could be made available to the community?

Other ideas?

FOCUS THEME: People and Demographics

Observe what kinds of people live, work, or walk on the street.

Get information from city hall about who lives and works in the area you are studying.

Create a questionnaire and interview people on the block.

Interview and profile or profiles of people who live or work on the block. How long have they lived there? What do they do for work? What are their favorite and least favorite aspects of the neighborhood? How has it changed during the time they have been there?

What different kinds of racial, ethnic, and socioeconomic groups live in the area? Has that changed over the years?

Make pie or bar graphs, or write out transcripts of interviews to illustrate your data.

Other ideas?

FOCUS THEME: Quality of Life

Interview residents about what they think are the best and worst features of the neighborhood.

Do a study of noise on the block.

Figure out how many people live on the block. Create a pie or bar graph to show density.

Create a new building, business, park, or community service to improve quality of life on the block.

Fill out a neighborhood report card for the area you are studying and the neighborhood where you live. Compare and contrast.

Other ideas?

FOCUS THEME: Retail and Business

Investigate the businesses that presently exist in your study area. How did they get there and whom do they serve?

Interview local business owners about what it's like to run a business in the area. Find out how and when they got started.

Research what kinds of jobs exist in the area. Who fills the available jobs, and how do they get them?

Find out how one would go about starting a new business in the area. Visit the chamber of commerce and/or the small business bureau.

Find out how one would go about getting financing for a new business. Talk to local bankers about what the process of applying for a small business loan entails.

Think of ideas for a new business you could locate in your study area. Do a marketing study of community needs to determine what kinds of new businesses or services are needed.

Other ideas?

FOCUS THEME: Transportation

Investigate what kinds of public transportation exist for people who live and work in the area.

Do a traffic assessment, recording the number of cars, busses, pedestrians, and cyclists at specific times during the day.

Interview people about how they commute to the area and get around the city in general. Do they feel the area is easily accessible? Why or why not?

Are businesses and sidewalks handicapped accessible? How does access affect people who live and work in the area?

Assess whether or not parking is a problem in the area.

Make suggestions for new transportation services needed in the area.

Other ideas?

FOCUS THEME: Zoning

Go to city hall or the office of community development to find out about zoning issues in your city.

Determine what building zone your study area is in. Do a zoning map of the area around the school.

Find out about the application process for a variance for non-compliant buildings.

Measure some buildings on the block to see if they meet their height and setback restrictions.

Other ideas?

STUDIO GROUP NAME

DATE

Focus Choice 1:

Focus Choice 2:

Focus Choice 3:

Proposal for Focus Theme Choice 1

Remember the who, what, and where questions and discuss both general and specific information you plan to gather.

Proposal for Focus Theme Choice 2

Proposal for Focus Theme Choice 3

Final Study Plan for Focus Theme

Once it has been determined which focus theme you and your home tean will investigate, you should further develop your team's ideas for a focus theme study plan. Describe in as much detail as possible exactly what study area you plan to focus on and why; whom you plan to interview and why; where you plan to visit; how you plan to present your findings; and what the timeline for your research activities will be.

Observing Your Study Area

Now it is time for you and your home team to begin to gather information.

Observation is an important part of the investigative process. You will begin by doing an observation exercise that requires a lot of concentration. You will each need to bring along a clipboard, a pencil, and an observation form to fill out. The first step is to go to your study area. You will have twenty minutes to walk around the area and take in everything that you can observe. Keep track of sights, sounds, shapes, smells, colors, buildings, types of people, trees, cars, and so on. Don't write anything down while you are walking; just observe.

At the end of twenty minutes, you will have another twenty minutes to write down everything you can remember about what you observed. You could draw a quick map to record your observations as well. When you go back to the classroom, you can compare notes with your fellow home team members about what stood out most for each of you.

Work with your home team to make a collective list of your observations, then go back to your study area and see how much more you are able to observe about the area now that your mind and senses have been stimulated by hearing about your teammates' observations.

NAME

DATE

THEME

OBSERVATION FORM

Observations:

■ Write a WorkLog entry describing your experience observing your study area. You can use the ideas below to guide your writing or write about other things that you have learned, discovered, and experienced.

OBSERVATION

■ Briefly describe the area your group studied. What did you observe?

■ How did it feel to observe a location in detail? How does that compare with walking through an area normally? (Do you usually pay attention to all your senses—sights, sounds, smells?)

EXERCISE:

■ What are some of the ways you got yourself to concentrate on detail?

■ How did your observations compare with the others in your group?

WORKLOG REFLECTION

■ When you returned to the study area, which of your observations and opinions changed? What new things did you notice?

■ What other situations in your life require you to observe in detail? What are possible future situations?

Mapping Your Study Area

Using the group mapping symbols your home team developed, map the five-block area your team has chosen as its study area. Before beginning, you will need to create a diagram of the streets located in your study area. The diagram should be large enough for you to record information including the location of buildings, businesses, houses, and other landmarks; significant outdoor spaces; street "furniture" such as benches, fire hydrants, and traffic lights and any other features you think are important to record. Your diagram should be drawn so that each street is accurately depicted in terms of scale and proportion. This can be achieved by enlarging a map of the area using a photocopy machine, or transposing the map to a larger scale.

The information you record on this map will serve as your field notes from which you will eventually be drawing a detailed map of your study area for your final presentation board.

Presentation Boards

After thoroughly investigating your study area, you and your teammates will put together all the information you have gathered and display it on presentation boards. Each group will be responsible for making two to four presentation boards. You can work individually or in pairs to make the different parts of the boards. At the end of the project, your whole group will present them to the rest of the class. Your presentation boards can show whatever information about your study area and focus theme you think is most interesting or important. However, as previously stated, the following information is required:

• A summary of your focus theme and its importance to the city

• Photographs that provide important visual information about your focus theme, the people you spoke with, and the sites you saw

• Typed interviews with people who have ideas and opinions about, or experience with, your focus theme

• Drawings illustrating some aspect of your focus theme

• A plan and symbol legend showing the location of the study area in relation to the school as well as important buildings or features of the area pertaining to the focus theme.

You are not limited to recording your information on presentation boards only. You might also make three-dimensional models of buildings or videotape interviews with people. All written material should be edited and typed (keyboarded). You can vary the size and font of text and headlines to make your presentation boards look more interesting and professional.

You can also tape various boards together to create stand-up or contiguous panels for your presentation, or you can mount your boards separately on the wall. Look at the handout labeled "sample layout" (see page 140) for ideas about how to put a board together. Before starting on your final boards, it is important that you think about all of the information your group plans to include and figure out how to best lay it out or arrange it on the boards. Do a pencil sketch of a number of different layout alternatives before deciding on a final scheme.

SAMPLE PRESENTATION BOARD LAYOUT

Theme Name and Title

General Information

Photos

Background Information

Written Observations

Location Map

Interviews

Photos

Group Names

Visual Observations

Drawings

Sample Questionnaire

Group Members in Action

Group Names

RESEARCH

■ Write a WorkLog entry describing your experience doing research on your study area and focus theme. You can use the ideas below to guide your writing or write about other things that you have learned, discovered, and experienced.

METHODS:

■ What were the first steps you took to research your study area and focus theme?

■ What tools and methods are you using to uncover information? For example, did you use the library? Where in the library did you look? Did you get help from a reference librarian? Did you make telephone calls? To where and to whom?

WORKLOG REFLECTION

■ What research strategies work best and why? How are you changing your research methods as you go along?

■ When researching your focus theme in your study area, what information are you having difficulty finding? Why is it difficult to gather that information? What can you do to meet those challenges?

NAME

DATE

WALKABOUT THE COMMUNITY

Describe some of the skills you learned while doing the WalkAbout activity (e.g., photography, interviewing, researching, drawing up plans, sketching pictures, etc.).

Description of Drawing
or Photograph

What were some of your team's most interesting findings while conducting research on your focus theme and study area?

Note: you can use this form or the free-write Portfolio Record form.

Who were some of the most interesting people you met during your research?

Were you pleased with your team's final presentation board? Why or why not? How did your group decide on the information you chose to display on the board?

Compare your oral and visual presentations. Which one did you find easier and why? Would you do anything differently to improve your oral or visual presentation?

WALKABOUT

- Write a WorkLog entry describing your experience of doing the WalkAbout the Community exercises and projects. You can use the ideas below to guide your writing, or write about other things you have learned, discovered, and experienced. ▬▬▬▬▬▬▬

THE COMMUNITY:

- The word "community" has different meanings for different people and situations. Write your own personal definition of community. ▬▬▬▬▬▬▬

- How would you describe your school's community? Write down ways to make the school function more like a community. ▬▬▬▬▬▬▬

- What role(s) do you think your school plays in its neighboring community? How could the school (as an institution) interact more with the community? How could students and school staff interact more with the community? Feel free to be imaginative and creative. You can even propose to change school rules and restrictions, if this would contribute to increasing the school's interactions with the community. ▬▬▬▬▬▬▬

WORKLOG REFLECTION

- How do personality, background, and interests influence observations in research and study?

- Describe a person you interviewed or met during your research for the presentation board. Rather than just rewriting the transcript or notes taken from the interview, try instead to write a personality profile of that person. You can start by considering these questions:

What were your first reactions to this person?	What other observations did you make about the person?
What did the person look like?	What qualities do you admire in this person?
How did he/she speak?	What qualities do you not admire?
What does the person do for work?	How does this person contribute to the community?
What does the person do besides work?	When will you have contact with this person again?

WalkAbout the Community:
Putting It All Together for Your CityWorks Portfolio

Now that you have finished the CityWorks unit entitled WalkAbout the Community, it is time to review the projects you have completed thus far, individually or as part of your home team, and continue to assemble records of the work you are organizing within your portfolio binder. These records can take the form of WorkLog reflections, Portfolio Record forms, photographs of projects, work samples, interviews, drawings, videotapes, computer disks (with stored project work)—anything that will communicate to others who you are, what you have done in City-Works, how you have done it, how you feel about it, and what you have learned in the process.

Remember to make sure that all of the written work included in your portfolio binder is edited. Both written and visual work should be well labeled and neatly presented. Below is a list of project work you should have completed during the WalkAbout the Community unit. If you need to write any missing WorkLog reflections or Portfolio Record forms if you would like to update or edit those that you have already completed, or if you need to put the finishing touches on any project work you plan to include in your portfolio binder as a work sample, take the time to do it now.

As you go through each of your products, review the six CityWorks goals listed on the Record of Accomplishment form you received as part of your packet of portfolio materials. Although each CityWorks activity corresponds to a particular CityWorks goal in terms of how the curriculum is organized, you will find that many of your products could be used as examples of a number of these goals. You should already have a cover sheet for each goal in your portfolio binder. As before, you may organize your work samples in whatever way you think makes most sense.

WalkAbout the Community Project List

What's a Neighborhood?

Neighborhood Report Cards

Symbols

Tour of Your Neighborhood

Mapping Your Block

Group Neighborhood Presentation Board

Neighborhoods: WorkLog Reflection

Investigating a Focus Theme

Choosing Your Focus Theme

Final Study Plan for a Focus Theme

Observing Your Study Area

Observation Exercise: WorkLog Reflection

Mapping Your Study Area

Presentation Boards

Research Methods: WorkLog Reflection

WalkAbout the Community: WorkLog Reflection

WalkAbout the Community: Portfolio Record Form

UNIT 3

Contributing to the Community

- UNIT 3 AT A GLANCE
- INTRODUCTION for the Teacher
- INTRODUCTION for the Student
- Contributing to the Community
- Putting it All Together for Your CityWorks Portfolio

INTRODUCTION FOR THE TEACHER

By the time students reach this third unit of City-Works, they will have developed most of the skills they will need for carrying out an extended community development project. They can draw on their familiarity with the design process (introduced in the various hands-on problems of Unit 1), as well as their experience investigating a community issue (in Unit 2), and presenting their findings in both visual and oral form (Units 1 and 2). Because of the ongoing emphasis on reflection and on working together as a team, they should know something about their own and each other's skills, interests and habits of work.

In Contributing to the Community students continue to learn about the community and themselves while applying what they have learned to addressing a real issue. The initial challenge of this unit is to select a community development problem that is meaningful to the students and "real enough" to attract the interest of adults who live and work in the community. The selection process allows students to draw on the thinking and research skills developed during the WalkAbout unit. Although each group tackled only one theme, the class collectively developed information on a range of community needs and resources. This unit will ask students to draw on this knowledge base while doing a more in-depth analysis of their neighborhoods.

Because many students may not be familiar with the notion of community development, it is important for them to meet with people who are responsible for local planning and development tasks. These adults can come in to give presentations about projects in which they are currently involved and can also play an important role responding to the students' own analyses of the resources and needs of the neighborhoods in which they live. To ensure a range of perspectives, the class might also interact with neighborhood activists and communi-ty representatives, whose views may differ from those of City Hall or the official community development department. The goal is for students to get a sense of what other people are working on "fixing" in the community, and ultimately, to think about what the class should and could contribute, given a realistic appraisal of their own skills and resources.

Throughout the process, teachers will face difficult choices about how directive to be and when. It may become clear early on in the class assessment of community needs and resources that a particular neighborhood has been slated for revitalization or redevelopment and that there is ferment and controversy in that neighborhood about the direction the development should take. Rather than spending several weeks in the assessment process, the teacher might decide to encourage the class to narrow their focus to this neighborhood and then, within that focus, to find a variety of ways to contribute to the debate. Or, a particular community agency or organization may approach the class with a field study on which they would like help, such as where to locate and how to develop plans for a heritage museum that would be attractive to local teens and their families as well as to tourists.

The point is to allow some room for student choice, whether in the form of a vote on the overall focus of the project or in the way actual tasks and assignments are apportioned. A good community development project will allow for multiple entry points and will benefit from many different kinds of contributions and products. (See p. 182 for guidelines).

Once an "umbrella" theme is selected, the class faces a second challenge: defining the products that will become the focus of the work students do in their small groups. For example, if the umbrella theme is the revitalization of a particular neighborhood, different groups might focus on a) developing

147

a scale model of a new building they are proposing for what is currently a vacant lot, b) creating display boards containing photographs and interviews with neighborhood heroes whose contributions should be recognized even as these changes are occurring, c) conducting a survey of teenagers in the high school who live in that neighborhood, soliciting their opinions about a range of issues connected to development, or d) surveying businesses in the area and developing their own plan for a new business.

Although the products worked on by student teams may be quite different from one another, all of the teams are expected to meet certain milestones or benchmarks along the way. The process begins with the team making a proposal, which they turn in to the teacher for review, followed by a period of research and investigation, culminating in the team producing a summary of what they learned. Then, the team focuses on actually making a product. Finally, there is an exhibition and oral presentation of the work. Whether the intended outcome is a three-dimensional scale model or a brochure for a historical walking tour, students are expected to proceed through all of these steps in the project cycle and to participate in an ongoing process of reflection and assessment.

This unit is the most public of the three parts of CityWorks. Although community experts and audiences become involved at many points during the course, it is during this unit that the most contact occurs, leading up to the culminating events of a community panel and an open house. Students will need feedback and assistance at various phases of the project cycle. It is particularly useful during this period for the teacher(s) to have the assistance of graduate student interns, paraprofessionals, and/or parents in putting these events together. Additional adults in the classroom allow for smaller and more focused teams of students. It is desirable for those adults who work with students to be able to commit to some kind of ongoing involvement over the ten- to twelve-week duration of the project.

Certainly there is a risk to students and teacher(s) alike in making the work so public. But this type of authentic assessment also encourages high-quality work. Knowing one's work will be viewed and questioned by experts and displayed to a large audience is a strong motivator in encouraging students to do a good job.

CONTRIBUTING TO THE COMMUNITY
Introduction

In the CityWorks Contributing to the Community unit you will have the opportunity to work with fellow students, teachers, and adults in your community to research and produce a wide variety of projects related to its development and improvement. In order to do this you will need to use many of the investigative research and production skills you practiced in the WalkAbout the Community exercise. It will also be important to establish relationships with professionals and neighborhood activists involved in community development. They can help you by sharing how they approach the work they do, what interesting projects they are currently working on, and how, as students, you might become involved in these projects in a meaningful way.

What is Community Development?

Community development is the process of actually improving a designated area of the city. Because many people live and work in a community, it is important for the planning process to be as participatory as possible, involving community development professionals, citizens, community groups, building developers, and local businesses in a collaborative effort to identify the community's unmet needs and then devise solutions for meeting them. The city's office of community development often works directly or indirectly with projects such as the design and creation of new buildings, roads and traffic systems, recreational facilities, outdoor spaces, public transportation systems, and services for the community.

In order to set the stage for you to work with your fellow students, teachers, and community partners in the creation of meaningful and dynamic community development projects, it will be necessary to establish relationships with the experts and local activists involved in the development of your community. Think about what questions you could ask these professionals to get to the core of what they do and how they approach their work. Go to visit them at their offices or invite them to give a presentation at your school and ask them to help you think about ways your CityWorks class might become involved in projects they are currently working on.

Here are some things you should make sure to find out about when you meet with them.

What is the range of projects they are involved in?

What projects could they describe to illustrate the process of taking a community project from start to finish?

How do they approach an analysis of community resources and needs?

What are their ideas about the community's most pressing needs?

What competing interests exist within the community?

How do they set priorities in terms of what types of projects they take on?

What part do local citizens play in setting priorities and making decisions for the community?

What community partners do they work with, and how is their relationship with these partners structured?

How much power do they ultimately have in deciding what does, or doesn't get built or developed in the community?

Creating a Neighborhood Resources and Needs Booklet

Before choosing a theme for your community development project, you will need to work together to identify and assess important community resources and needs. In this activity you may work individually or in groups to do an analysis of the resources and the needs of the neighborhood in which you live. Your findings should be compiled in a booklet format and must include the following items:

A locator map highlighting existing resources in your neighborhood. (You can use the neighborhood map you created during the WalkAbout the Community activity or create a new map of your neighborhood indicating the location of its main streets, outdoor spaces, public buildings, and important landmarks.)

A summary of your own thoughts about the existing resources you appreciate now and those you would like to see improved upon or introduced.

Write-ups of interviews with at least three people who live and/or work in your neighborhood describing their opinions about the neighborhood's resources and needs.

Other information obtained from observation, reading local newspapers, contacting neighborhood groups (such as zoning committees and crime watch groups), or talking to local residents.

The written information you gather for your Neighborhood Needs and Resources Booklet should be typed and edited. You may also create a cover for your booklet and/or include photos, drawings, and any other visual information. Make sure all written and visual information is clearly labeled and laid out.

Once you have completed your Neighborhood Resources and Needs Booklets, present them to the larger group and take note of the common elements and themes that reappear as important community needs. These elements will provide a good starting point for the identification of an "umbrella" theme for the group's community development project.

When thinking about your neighborhood's existing resources and unmet needs, refer to the following list of Community Development Themes, first introduced in the WalkAbout activity.

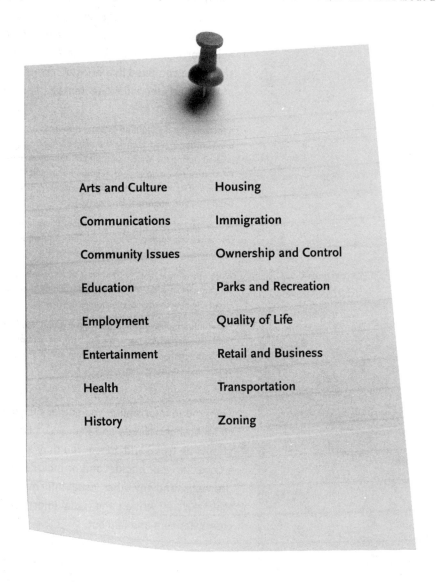

Arts and Culture	Housing
Communications	Immigration
Community Issues	Ownership and Control
Education	Parks and Recreation
Employment	Quality of Life
Entertainment	Retail and Business
Health	Transportation
History	Zoning

Envisioning a Theme for Your Community Development Project

The theme your group chooses to focus on for their community development project should be broad enough to allow for the creation of a wide range of discrete projects and activities that will be interesting to students and teachers, yet still fall under some kind of unifying "umbrella." For instance, if better public transportation came up repeatedly as a need articulated by students and neighborhood residents, it could serve as the organizing theme for the group's community development project. It is also possible for the larger group to focus on investigating or revitalizing a particular neighborhood in the community. In both of these instances, smaller project groups could identify and pursue related areas of more specific interest. At various points during the unit, these discrete projects will come together for presentation and exhibition.

Identifying possible themes for your project will require that you work together with fellow students as well as with teachers and community representatives. Invite community representatives and community development professionals into the school and share with them the information you gathered while researching your own neighborhoods. Ask for their suggestions and ideas about the community's areas of greatest need. You can also organize a brainstorming session involving a wide range of people with varying needs and outlooks.

It is often most interesting for groups to become involved in real projects within the community. These may be projects slated for future development but already under way in some form or another. Choosing authentic projects makes it easier to find adults in the community who are already actively involved (and have an interest in getting you involved) in the project. Look to these adults to give you ongoing feedback about your ideas and projects as they develop. If the project your group chooses is hypothetical, you can make it "real" in the sense that it is a plausible concept you approach in a realistic way. In this case, your group should still try and bring in community partners who will assist you in directing and evaluating the work you decide to take on.

Finally, the project you choose should provide multiple entry points to spark the interest of students and teachers alike. Use your imaginations to weave in activities playing on the strengths and interests of the group while providing opportunities for hands-on learning, creative problem-solving, and academic skill building.

The Phases of the CityWorks Community Development Project

Note: During the CityWorks Community Development Unit, you will be part of small groups of 8 to 10 students working to develop projects arising from authentic community issues and needs. In order for you to do focused and high-quality work, you will need to work well together as a team and have access to an adult facilitator to direct your work and give you feedback on a regular basis. The facilitator of your group may be a teacher, a parent, a student teacher, a graduate student, or an interested adult from the community. In addition to a group facilitator, you may invite other adults as expert advisors to assist you with particular aspects of your research and investigation.

Phase 1: Project Identification

In this phase, the whole class first works together to identify an "umbrella theme" for the project, then defines a variety of smaller group projects emanating from it. This phase should take into consideration the information you gathered during the creation of your Neighborhood Needs and Resources Booklet," as well as suggestions from the local community development professionals with whom you spoke. Try to choose a theme relating to community development projects that are currently in the planning or execution stages. This will create opportunities to link up with community organizations that are also working on the project and may want some help or input from teens. Smaller group projects should relate in some way to the umbrella theme and play upon the interests and abilities of students and teachers.

FOR EXAMPLE, deciding on a unifying umbrella theme such as Housing in the Community could lead you to generate ideas for small group projects such as the development of a video documentary or oral history project about the effect of housing and demographic changes on longtime residents of the community; a brochure/guide describing housing types found in the community that represent different periods of history; a booklet highlighting the process one goes through to buy a house; a study of the housing needs of community members and how well they are being met; architectural design drawings and models for new housing prototypes; and a business plan for a new housing construction enterprise.

Phase 2: Research and Investigation

Once a range of smaller group projects have been identified, you will choose which project(s) you would like to work on and begin the process of identifying and gathering the information you will need to develop your ideas more fully. The research and investigation methods you use will vary from group to group, depending on the specific focus of your project. This phase will require you to tap into available community contacts and resources and to think through the methods you plan to use to gather, evaluate, and present your data. In this phase of the project, it is important that you look to community partners and to your teachers for the guidance and skill training required for your group to do high-level work.

FOR EXAMPLE, if your group decides to work on a video documentary or oral history project about longtime residents of the city, you might visit the local historical society, library, or city hall to gather general information about how the housing situation and demographics of the city have changed over time, then interview elderly residents about their actual experiences. Your group would have to decide what kind of data to gather, including video footage, photographs, transcribed interviews, and written observations. If your group decides to work on architectural designs and models for new housing, you would have to research housing prototypes in architectural magazines as well as learn about working with architectural scale and drawing conventions. Your group might interview local architects who have designed housing for the community or do a study of available parcels of land that could be developed for housing. Finally, a group working to create a business plan for a new construction company would likely want to talk to local contractors about how they got started and how they run their businesses. You might also visit the local chamber of commerce, small business bureau, or bank to find out what's involved in starting a business and whom your competition would be.

Phase 3: Production

In this phase, your group will present its findings, using a wide variety of media, including written material, brochures, statistical charts, models and drawings, and/or video documentaries. Obviously, the range of your products will be limited by the resources available. It is important that your group seek out the correct materials with which to fashion its products, and obtain guidance in how to create them.

FOR EXAMPLE, a study of longtime residents may take the form of a video documentary, if the equipment and video editing capacity exists at your school, or it could be written up as an illustrated paper or booklet. Your group would also need to think about the audience for your video or booklet, how many copies you would need to generate, and what venues would be good for its distribution. Meanwhile, if your group were producing architectural models and drawings of housing prototypes, it would need access to the necessary drafting and model-making tools and materials as well as training in their use. A group researching the creation of a construction business might make the choice to publish the bulk of its findings in a report format but then decide to produce a business name, identity, logo, and advertising campaign as well.

Phase 4: Exhibition and Presentation

In this phase, your project group will present its ideas, findings, and products to an audience of its peers as well as to appropriate professionals and community groups. These presentations will give your group valuable feedback on the work it is doing and should occur at various phases of the project's development. To the extent that your project addresses authentic community needs and issues, it may generate participation on the part of adults in the community who have a genuine interest in your findings and who are in a position to give you advice about the scope and content of your investigations.

At the end of the Community Development unit, a large final exhibition and open house should be held to showcase your work. It is at this time that the umbrella theme comes fully to life, as projects are seen in relationship to one another and a synergistic effect is achieved where the whole becomes greater than the sum of its parts. The open house should be built up as an important and exciting event, open to the school community, the larger community, the press and other media representatives, special interest and community groups, and a panel of "expert" professionals who will critique your work.

FOR EXAMPLE, the project group completing a study on longtime residents would want to make sure that the "expert panel" included an elderly resident of the city, an employee from the city's office of housing and development, and/or a video producer. The group exhibiting drawings and models of housing prototypes could also invite a housing expert as well s a local architect. The group developing a business plan for a construction company would want to invite local contractors, builders, or representatives from the city's building department to sit on the panel.

Sample Community Development Projects

For a community development topic to keep students engaged, interested, and productive for several months, it needs to meet the test of being "real enough." The best way to meet that criteria is to provide assistance or consultation to a real "client," such as the department of community development, the mayor's office, or a local tourism agency. The examples below, drawn from the CityWorks program at the Rindge School of Technical Arts in Cambridge, Massachusetts, illustrate how an issue being tackled by people in the community can provide a starting point for a number of connected projects that are achievable by a team of students.

Example 1: Planning a Local Discovery Museum

This project theme is most relevant in a community in which tourism is a major industry. In the community development project, students become involved in planning the museum and/or exhibits for it. The project provides opportunities for them to learn more about local history and resources and, at the same time, to contribute to the city in an important way.

Before selecting specific topics for projects, students engage in a series of introductory activities, including 1) talking with staff from the local office of community development to find out how they approach this kind of development project as well as how the city has changed in the past 100 years; 2) consulting with the local tourist board or companies that run local tourism services; and 3) taking a field trip to a nearby historical museum or national park to look at the kinds of exhibits and how they are put together and displayed.

Project Groups

The following project groups all work towards different aspects of creating the building exhibits, tours, and activities for the Discovery Museum.

Walking Tours

Students research and put together walking tours of the area. The tours may be specifically designed for teenagers visiting the area and should be presented in a professional brochure format that can be distributed at a local tourist information booth. Some ideas for tour topics include 1) points of interest for teenagers visiting the city (where teenagers can shop, eat, and hang out); 2) fun things to do when visiting the area with children; 3) where to find the best ethnic restaurants and how these relate to the major ethnic groups of the community; 4) a walk through the history of the community.

Designing the Museum

Students explore possible sites for the location of the Discovery Museum. This works best if a local tourism agency or business is acting as the group's client and gives them information about all the features the building must have. The group works together to design a building and site plan for the museum and builds scale models of the proposed building.

A People's History: Changes Through Struggle

Students create a local-history exhibit on a time when change was achieved through struggle. Issues to be investigated could include the struggles for good schooling, civil rights, neighborhood safety, or rent control. The group puts together a display board and video documentary.

Studio Fronts: Building a City in the Classroom

Students build studio fronts in the CityWorks classroom, each designed to represent a typical type of architecture in the local area. The overall visual effect to strive for is the look of the city within the classroom. In addition to building the fronts, students investigate and put together a display about old and new building details and how construction has changed over the past 100 years. The display should be of exhibit quality.

The High School: Past, Present, and Future

Students create an exhibit which looks at the high school itself, from its founding to the present. Using old and new photographs, yearbooks, school newspapers, and interviews with alumni and teachers, students gather information about how the school has changed (in terms of demography, physical plant, rules, programming, courses, and extracurricular activities. In addition, students might want to look into topics of high interest such as the history of its sports teams and the changes in teen culture and fashion. The group also puts together sketches and stories about the high school of the future, based on how they think school and workplaces may change in the next twenty years.

Ethnic Recipes and Remedies

Students look at some of the ethnic groups that have settled in the city and investigate their various styles of cooking and their home remedies for common ailments. They obtain old family recipes and remedies through interviews at home and with elders in the community, collecting all of these into a booklet that could be distributed through the museum. Students also prepare some of the dishes for special luncheons for elders in the community and the final exhibit in June.

Marketing the Museum

Students work on graphic design projects for the Discovery Museum, which include creating a T-shirt depicting an important feature of their community, designing and producing a logo for the museum, creating a large wall map of the city, helping to put together high-quality brochures for the walking tours, and doing other design work that comes up as the ideas for the museum are developed. The group tries to sell its silk screen for the T-shirt to a local store.

Water Works

Students investigate water in the city: where it comes from, how it is protected from pollutants, how it is used in industry, how it is used by the fire department, and how it is treated to make it safe to drink. The group takes field trips to the water department and puts together an interactive exhibit explaining and demonstrating the water treatment process.

19

19

19

Example 2: Teen Visions for a Revitalized Neighborhood

This umbrella theme can work in any community. It can also be used over a period of several years, with a different neighborhood of the city as the focus each year. The input of young people is important in any effort the city is making to improve its neighborhoods. Community and neighborhood organizations, the department of community development and/or the Mayor's office are all potential collaborators or clients for this project.

Teen Visions Survey

Students work with a neighborhood group to compose a questionnaire for teens about their ideas for improving the neighborhood. After administering the questionnaire to several hundred students in the high school, they create a computer database to help them input, analyze, graph, and display their findings. They present their findings at a meeting of the neighborhood group for comments and feedback.

New Designs for the Neighborhood

Students develop designs and build architectural models of new buildings to be located in any vacant lots in the neighborhood (or, if there are no vacant lots, on the site of buildings slated for demolition). Students choose the type of building they would like to design based on their assessment of community needs. They learn the steps one goes through to design an actual building and visit local architects involved in the development of this neighborhood.

Electronic Map

Students build a Plexiglass map of the neighborhood, color-coded and wired to light up key landmarks. The map can show existing landmarks, services, and key locations, as well as student ideas for new businesses, services, and outdoor recreation spaces aimed at revitalizing the area.

Grandma's Place Restaurant

Students meet senior citizens in the area to record their favorite recipes as well as memories about their lives living in this area. They practice cooking the recipes, make a cookbook, and prepare a meal for seniors. Students also develop a plan and model for a new restaurant that would serve this type of menu to be located in the neighborhood of the study.

A Look at Future Transportation

Students develop designs and a model for an electric vehicle-charging station to be located at an appropriate garage or parking area in the neighborhood. They create a business plan for "while-you-park" charging and inspection of gasoline-powered cars. Students also create an exhibit on the latest advances in electric car technology and how they will affect the city.

The Many Faces of Our Neighborhood: A Video Documentary

Students create a video documentary about the neighborhood, based on interviews with a variety of people who live and work there. They focus on the multicultural flavor of the community; how longtime residents feel about the area and the changes it has gone through over the years; and what changes they would like to see take place in the future. The same group, or a different group of students can also use enlarged photographs of the people, and shortened versions of their interviews to create a visual display for the city hall.

Teen Tours

Students research and design a brochure highlighting the best places in the area for teens to shop, eat, have fun, and hang out. The tours should be presented in a professional brochure format that can be distributed at a local tourist information booth. Simple business plans may also be developed for new services or businesses catering to teenagers.

Teen Visions: A Graphic Identity Project

Students design a logo and graphic identity for the Teen Visions Project. They create information sheets about each of the different community groups involved in the revitalization process and print a T-shirt with the project logo. They can try to sell the silk screen to a local store for additional distribution.

Guidelines for a Successful Community Development Project
A successful community development project:

Addresses an authentic need in the community

Allows multiple entry points

Is manageable within given time frames, skill sets, and resource levels

Articulates milestones to keep students on track

Assures that "experts" spend real time interacting with students

Provides feedback loop for students to assess and rethink their work

Results in final products and presentations to promote a sense of completion

Provides an interested audience for the work

Presenting to a Panel of Community Experts

At the end of the CityWorks Community Development Project, your team will present their work to an audience including a panel of community experts, fellow students, teachers, parents, and other members of the school community. The purpose of these presentations is for you to showcase your work and to get valuable feedback and advice, particularly from adults who have expertise in the areas you have studied. The expert panel can include activists and community development professionals who have been involved with the project from its inception as well as other community members whom you talked to or met during your research.

You should present your projects using the best medium for communicating your ideas and your findings. Presentations may include presentation boards, architectural models, drawings, brochures, photos, videos, and any other products the team has created.

Prepare carefully for your presentations, making sure your presentation boards and other products are finished on time. You should also create presentation outlines and practice your presentations. Watching a videotape of your team practicing their presentation and discussing it in the group can be an excellent way to improve your presentation skills. All team members are encouraged to participate in your team's presentation, with each of you taking responsibility for some aspect of the information to be communicated. After presenting your projects, be prepared to answer questions from the expert panel and the audience.

The panel of community experts should be assembled early in the project. In fact, it is much more effective if panelists are able to give you feedback at various stages of your project's development: at the beginning; the midpoint; and the final exhibition. In that way, you will have the opportunity to respond to their suggestions and comments as you develop your projects.

Tips for Putting Together the Community Development Exhibition and Open House

In order to put together a successful exhibition and open house, students and teachers will need to prepare in the following ways:

- Generate lots of energy and enthusiasm about the event among students and teachers. The open house is a celebration of all of the hard work you have been doing.
- Invite parents and siblings. Make sure to have invitations translated into appropriate languages and follow up with phone calls by teachers to get parents on board. Send the invitations out at least one month in advance to allow parents time to schedule for the event. Include "save the date" cards they can keep as a reminder.

- Invite community partners and members of the larger community. The more people the better. Develop a mailing list you can add to from year to year that includes city officials, the school board, professional groups, and representatives from community organizations.

- Develop a memorable graphic or logo identity for the community development theme and plaster it everywhere: on invitations, posters, T-shirts, and newsletters.

- Contact the local press to let them know the open house will provide lots of good issues to cover, as well as great photo opportunities. Have them do a pre-exhibition article to advertise the open house.

- Find the appropriate exhibition space with a large area for group presentations and exhibits and smaller areas or additional wall space for related exhibits.

- Make sure you have materials such as poster board, markers, colored paper, and cardboard with which to prepare professional-looking presentation boards.

- Set high standards for the presentation of project work, including clear graphic layout and thorough labeling of products and exhibition boards.

- Think "multimedia." Try to use varied presentation formats, including video images, slide presentations, overheads, PowerPoint presentations, three-dimensional models, and two-dimensional presentation boards. Plan carefully to make sure you have all of the audiovisual equipment you need.

- Put together an "expert panel" of community representatives with strong professional interests in, or connections to, the various aspects of the project. Send panelists a summary of all the projects they will be viewing before they arrive at the presentation. Allow ample time for presentations and a question and answer period for each group presenting.

- Make sure you are fully prepared for your project presentations. Preparations should include videotaped practice presentations and feedback sessions.

- Decide on a date for the exhibit that doesn't compete with other school events occurring at the end of the semester or school year.

- Identify students to act as guides, offering guided tours of the exhibit.

- Arrange to have food and/or music at the event if possible.

- Enlist the help of students and teachers in setting up and cleaning up the exhibit and presentation area.

- Create a floor plan and/or clearly understandable signage system to help visitors navigate the exhibit.

RESEARCHING

- Write about your experiences researching your community development focus theme. You can use the ideas below to guide your thoughts, or you can write about other things you learned, discovered, or explored. ▬▬▬▬▬▬▬▬▬▬▬▬▬

- What research methods are proving most fruitful in analyzing your community and researching your particular focus for the community development project? Why? ▬▬▬▬▬▬

YOUR PROJECT:

- Do you think that your group's focus is a good one? Why or why not? What kinds of information have you been able to find from your research? ▬▬▬▬▬▬▬▬▬

- Which research methods and skills from the WalkAbout are you using again? ▬▬▬▬▬

- What research skills and methods do you foresee using for the duration of the project? What new skills will you need to learn? ▬▬▬▬▬▬▬▬▬

WORKLOG REFLECTION

- How are you recording your research? Are you finding this method effective? Have you compared your methods with other students? ▬▬▬▬▬▬▬▬

- What obstacles are you encountering in obtaining resources or solving problems? What are some things you can do to overcome these obstacles? ▬▬▬▬▬▬▬

CONTRIBUTING

- Write about your experiences doing a community development project. You can use the ideas below to guide your thoughts, or you can write about other things you learned, discovered, or explored.

- What real need in the community did your project address? How did it address this need?

TO THE

- In what new ways do you now think about your community and its needs?

- Can you think of other projects you'd like to tackle in the future to act upon those needs and influence the community?

COMMUNITY:

- How has your personal definition of community changed during this unit?

- Did you establish a friendship or friendly acquaintance with any of the expert panel members or any adults you encountered during research? What did you learn from this person? How did having personal contact and communication with them affect your work?

WORKLOG REFLECTION

- Write the story of your project, from start to finish.

NAME

DATE

PORTFOLIO RECORD

CONTRIBUTING TO THE COMMUNITY

Description of Drawing or Photograph

Describe the community development project you and your group worked on.

Glue photograph or drawing
of your community development
project here.

Note: you can use this form or the free-write Portfolio Record form.

What skills did you need to learn to complete your projects? Which skills did you enjoy learning the most? The least? Why?

Describe your team's presentation. How did you present your findings and what role did you play in the presentation?

What feedback from the expert panel did you find most helpful and why?

What role did you play in organizing and participating in the open house and exhibition? Did you think that the open house was a success? Why or why not?

Contributing to the Community: Putting It All Together

Now that you have finished the CityWorks unit Contributing to the Community, it is time to review the projects you have completed thus far, individually or as part of your home team, and finish assembling the records of your work you are organizing within your portfolio binder. These records can take the form of WorkLog reflections, Portfolio Record forms, photographs of projects, work samples, interviews, drawings, videotapes, computer disks (with stored project work)—anything that will communicate to others who you are, what you have done in CityWorks, how you have done it, how you feel about it, and what you learned in the process.

Remember to make sure that all of the written work included in your portfolio binder is edited. Both written and visual work should be well labeled and neatly presented. Below is a list of project work you should have completed during the Contributing to the Community unit. If you need to write any missing WorkLog reflections or Portfolio Record forms, if you would like to update or edit those you have already completed, or if you need to put the finishing touches on any project work you plan to include in your portfolio binder as a work sample, take the time to do it now.

As you go through each of your products, review the six CityWorks goals listed on the Record of Accomplishment form you received as part of your packet of portfolio materials (see page 189). Although each CityWorks activity corresponds to a particular CityWorks goal in terms of how the curriculum is organized, you will find that many of your products could be used as examples of a number of these goals. You should have a cover sheet for each goal already in your portfolio binder. As before, you may organize your work samples in any way you think makes most sense.

Project List:

What is Community Development?

Creating a Neighborhood Resources and Needs Booklet

Neighborhood Resources and Needs: WorkLog Reflection

Envisioning a Theme for Your Community Development Project

Project Identification Phase

Research and Investigation Phase

Production Phase

Exhibition and Presentation Phase

Presenting to a Panel of Community Experts

Researching Your Project: WorkLog Reflection

Contributing to the Community: WorkLog Reflection

Contributing to the Community: Portfolio Record Form

Resources: Organizations and Publications

The American Architectural Foundation (AAF) of the American Institute of Architects (AIA)
1735 New York Avenue NW
Washington, DC 20006
(202) 626-7573
Web site: www.aia.org/
Alan Sandler, Director of Public Education

The AAF's education program, *Learning By Design*, provides resources to assist teachers in developing practical activities for students to learn about their physical surroundings. AAF materials include a reference book of environmental education resources; teaching units on various disciplines from the perspective of architecture; and a network of architect/educators who disseminate information about *Learning By Design* and assist with projects. In addition, many local AIA chapters provide schools with architecture- and design-based curricula.

Architectural Education Resource Center (AERC)
131 Hillside Road
Franklin, MA 02038
(508) 528-4517
e-mail: aerc@norfolk-county.com
Jan Ham, Director
Web site: www.norfolk-county.com/aerc

AERC programs and materials encourage children to use the architectural design process to express their ideas and provide teachers with the support and training to build community-based, multidisciplinary design projects into their curricula. AERC offers professional development workshops for K-12 teachers; children's enrichment programs for grades 2 through 8; and a variety of other materials and resources.

Autodesk Foundation
11 McInnis Parkway
San Rafael, California 94903
(415) 507-5000; fax (415) 507-6339
Web site: www.autodesk.com/foundation/

The Autodesk Foundation helps to further school reform by supporting whole-school change and widely disseminating information on project-based and school-to-career learning. The Foundation holds an annual Project-Based Learning Conference. For more information on the conference, visit the Autodesk Foundation Web site. Autodesk also runs a monthly e-mail newsletter for educators and others interested in project-based learning, school-to-career initiatives, and school reform. To subscribe to this newsletter, send e-mail to: listserv@peach.ease.lsoft.com
In the body of the message type only: subscribe PBLNEWS first name, last name

Center for Environmental Design and Education
College of Architecture and Urban Planning
The University Of Washington
208T Gould Hall
Seattle, Washington 98195-5726
(206) 685-3361

Dr. Sharon E. Sutton, FAIA, Director
The Center assists in the design of K-12 learning environments, the development of K-12 place-related curricula, and in the dissemination of practice and research innovations in these two areas.

Center for City Building Education (CBE)
2210 Wilshire Boulevard, #303
Santa Monica, CA 90403
(310) 471-0090; fax (310) 471-1955
Doreen Nelson, Director

The CBE methodology for elementary and secondary teachers demonstrates how design and creativity enhance and extend the teaching of math, sciences, language arts, and social studies. Students in CBE programs construct a city of the future in their classroom to unlock and speed up their creative thinking skills. CBE creates and distributes several print, video, and multimedia publications.

Center for Understanding the Built Environment (CUBE)
5328 West 67th Street
Prairie Village, KS 66208
(913) 262-0691; fax (913) 262-8546
e-mail: ginny@cubekc.org
Web site: www.cubekc.org/
Ginny Graves, Director

CUBE brings together educators with community partners to improve and synergize the built and natural environment of cities. Through CUBE educational programs, children learn problem-solving and social skills, the value of the built environment, and how to take responsible action in the community. CUBE offers many educational materials in print, CD-ROM, film, and video format. Relevant products available from CUBE: *The Box City Curriculum* teaches how cities are planned or unplanned; what makes a quality city, and how citizens can participate in the improvement of the built environment. *Walk Around the Block* is a workbook that guides students in using their neighborhoods and cities as a way to understand architectural design, city planning, preservation, history, economics, politics, geography, science, and art. *My Backyard History*, a workbook by David Weitzman, leads children in the creation of an oral and written history of their neighborhoods and families.

City/Build

Historic Neighborhoods Foundation
99 Bedford Street
Boston, MA 02111
(617) 426-1885
e-mail: hnf@thecia.net
Nina Meyer, Director

City/Build offers Boston area high school students hands-on, real-world opportunities to learn design, urban planning, and construction by partnering with a local business or organization. City/Build molds their curriculum to fit the needs of schools and classrooms.

Coalition of Essential Schools (CES)

1814 Franklin Street
Suite 700
Oakland, CA 94612
(510) 433-1451; fax (510) 433-1455
Web site: www.essentialschools.org

The Coalition is an international school reform movement founded by Ted Sizer. Its ten Common Principles serve as guidelines for school people in rethinking their approach to teaching and learning. Contact CES for a copy of their extensive publications list. Relevant publications available from CES: Allen, David and Joseph MacDonald, "Keeping Student Performance Central: The New York Assessment Collection." Niguidula, David, "The Digital Portfolio: A Richer Picture of Student Performance."

The Community Service-Learning Institute

Slippery Rock University, Slippery Rock, Pennsylvania
214 Spotts World Culture Building
Slippery Rock, Pennsylvania 16057
(412) 738-CARE; fax (412) 738-2314
e-mail: csli@sru.edu
Web site: www.sru.edu/depts/artsci/gov/csli/service.htm

The institute provides and coordinates training and technical assistance, professional development, curricular and co-curricular development, research, model programs, special events in all areas of service-learning and community service for K-12 students, school faculty, social service agency staff, and community members.

Education Development Center (EDC)

55 Chapel Street
Newton, MA 02160
(800) 225-4276
Web site: www.edc.org

EDC conducts research and develops programs in a wide range of areas including K-12 education and institu-

tional reform. Contact EDC for a copy of their extensive publications list. Relevant publications available from EDC include: *Designing Spaces: Visualizing, Planning and Building* (1995). Students use geometry to analyze buildings from around the world and design model houses (middle school). *From the Ground Up: Modeling, Measuring, and Constructing Houses* (1993). Students use scale, measurements, nets, and geometry constructions to build a model house (middle school). *Structures: Insights, Elementary Hands-on Inquiry Science Curriculum* (1994).

Expeditionary Learning Outward Bound (ELOB)

122 Mount Auburn Street
Cambridge, MA 02138
(617) 576-1260; fax (617) 576-1340
e-mail: Meg@elob.ci.net
Web site: http://hugse1.harvard.edu/~elob/elobpage.htm

ELOB offers a curriculum centered on "learning expeditions" developed by teachers in their schools. The curriculum involves challenge, teamwork, and learning by doing, and requires flexible block scheduling, heterogeneous grouping, and multi-year student-teacher assignments.

Facing History and Ourselves

16 Hurd Road
Brookline, MA 02146
(617) 232-1595
e-mail: Cathy@facing.org

Facing History is a national educational and teacher training organization that engages students in an examination of racism, prejudice, and anti-Semitism. By studying the historical development and lessons of the Holocaust and other examples of genocide, students make connections between history and the moral choices they confront in their own lives. Contact Facing History for a copy of their extensive publications list.

Foundation for Architecture
One Penn Center at Suburban Station
Suite 1165
Philadelphia, PA 19103
(215) 569-3187; fax (215) 569-4688
Rolaine Copeland, Marcy Abrams
Web site: www.voicenet.com/~ffa

The Foundation for Architecture holds workshops for teachers and group leaders interested in integrating architecture and the built environment into their existing program. The Foundation also maintains a Resource Center that houses and distributes curriculum research information, activity workbooks, audiovisual materials, teaching kits, building materials, and more.

Foxfire Fund, Inc.
P.O. Box 541
Mountain City, GA 30562-0541
(706) 746-5828; fax (706) 746-5829
Web site: www.foxfire.org/

Foxfire is a national nonprofit education organization that proposes innovative approaches to teaching and learning, provides a framework for developing active, collaborative, learner-centered environments, and promotes continuous interaction between students and their communities. Foxfire works with educators, primarily through teacher-training and support programs, to redefine the relationship among teachers, learners, and the cur-

riculum. *The Foxfire Magazine* is managed and operated by the students at Rabun County High School in grades 9 through 12, and can be viewed online at: www.geocities.com/Athens/Acropolis/9072/main.html

The George Lucas Educational Foundation (GLEF)
PO Box 3494
San Rafael, CA 94912
(415) 662-1600; fax (415) 662-1605
e-mail: edutopia@glef.org
Web site: http://glef.org/

GLEF gathers, synthesizes, and disseminates information in several media to promote and support school change and share strategies for improving schools, especially those that integrate technology with teaching and learning.

Hands and Minds, Inc.
23 Donnell Street
Cambridge, MA 02138
(617) 864-1771

Hands and Minds staff, under a grant from the U.S. Department of Vocational and Adult Education, headed the New Urban High School (NUHS) Project, a national initiative for school change. NUHS worked with six high schools that have developed whole-school designs for linking school with the adult world and for connecting with broader reform initiatives. Publications available from Hands and Minds: Berman, Tamara, and Adria Steinberg. *The Via Book: A Best Practices Manual From The Vocational Integration With Academics Project at the Rindge School of Technical Arts.* Cambridge (1997) *The New Urban*

High School Practitioner's Guide: Case Studies and Practitioner Materials (1998).

Industrial Designers Society of America (IDSA)
1142 Walker Road
Great Falls, VA 22066
(703) 759-0100

IDSA provides information on the field of industrial design to teachers, including a journal devoted to teaching design to children.

Jobs for the Future (JFF)
88 Broad Street, 8th Floor
Boston, MA 02110
(617) 728-4446; fax (617) 728-4857
e-mail: info@jff.org
Web site: www.jff.org

JFF works nationally with schools, districts, and communities to integrate real-world standards, authentic problems, and community resources into instructional practice and to mobilize employers and other community allies to increase access to higher education and high-skilled employment. Contact JFF for their extensive publications list. Relevant publications available from JFF: Allen, Lili, Christopher Hogan, and Adria Steinberg. "Knowing and Doing: Connecting Learning and Work." Providence, RI: Northeast and Islands Regional Education Laboratory at Brown University. For more information contact Deborah Collins, Director of Research and Development, LAB, tel: 800-521-9550, x.260 or e-mail: d_collins@brown.edu
Cushman, Kathleen, Adria Steinberg, and Rob Riordan. "Rigor and Relevance: Essential Ideas About Connect-

ing School and Work" (1998). "Focus on Freshmen: An Energetic, Hands-On Curriculum for Developing Successful High School Students" (1996). Goldberger, Sue, and Richard Kazis. "Revitalizing High Schools: What the School-to-Career Movement Can Contribute" (1995). *School-to-Work Toolkit: Building a Local Program* (1994). Steinberg, Adria. *Real Learning, Real Work: School-to-Work as High School Reform.* New York: Routledge, 1997. (CityWorks is featured in several chapters in *Real Learning, Real Work.* For an additional account of City-Works, see "Beyond the Shop: Reinventing Vocational Education," by Larry Rosenstock and Adria Steinberg, in *Democratic Schools,* eds. Michael W. Apple, James A. Beane. Alexandria: ASCD, 1995).

MICROSOCIETY, Inc. (MSI)

306 Cherry Street
Suite 200
Philadelphia, PA 19106
Executive Director: Carolynn King
(215) 922-4006
Web site: www.microsociety.org/

MSI provides elementary and middle school practitioners with teaching techniques and motivational tools that prepare children for the real world outside the classroom. A MicroSociety® (program school is a miniature community created and run by students. Children oversee businesses and cultural institutions, courts, and legislatures.

Salvadori Educational Center on the Built Environment (SECBE)

City College of New York
Harris Hall Room 202
138th Street and Convent Avenue
New York, NY 10031
(212) 650-5497; fax (212) 650-5546

The SECBE is an innovative program for teaching mathematics and science to young people through compelling hands-on activities involving architecture and engineering. The Center offers books and materials that can be used in K-12 and beyond.

TERC Communications

2067 Massachusetts Avenue
Cambridge, MA 02140
(617) 547-0430; fax (617) 349-3535
e-mail: info@terc.edu
Web site: www.terc.edu/

TERC is a nonprofit research and development organization committed to improving mathematics and science learning and teaching. TERC creates innovative curricula, fosters teacher professional development, pioneers creative uses of technology in education, and aims to develop equitable opportunities for underserved learners. Contact TERC for more information about their many products and publications. An example of a starter TERC product is Mapping Our City; with TERC's assistance and support, middle school students and teachers in Boston use computerized maps and interactive software tools called Geographic Information Systems (GIS) to explore their urban community. Mapping Our City Web site: http://tea-party.terc.edu/gis/MapCity/moc-terc.html

Resources: Web Sites

This is a partial listing of the many Web sites dedicated to service learning, oral history, and community exploration.

Americorps Home Page
www.cns.gov/americorps/index.html

AmeriCorps is a national service program that allows people of all ages and backgrounds to earn help paying for their education in exchange for a year of service. AmeriCorps members meet community needs with services that range from housing renovation to child immunization to neighborhood policing. The Americorps Web site provides Internet links to many other service-related sites. See especially The Learn & Serve America Home Page on the Americorps site. Learn and Serve America is a grants program that supports teachers and community members who involve young people in service that relates to studies in school.

The Enterprise School
www.enterpriseschool.com
Michele Surwit, Principal
e-mail: msurwit@worldnet.att.net

This Web site explains the Enterprise school's unique program of community service, internships, apprenticeships, and an onsite simulated professional business environment.

"Just"
www.libertynet.org/~just/wilma/list.cgi/ct3

"Just" provides links to thirty-five oral history sites that themselves contain resources, examples of oral history projects, and how-to instruction for oral history of different communities and cultures.

National Service-Learning Cooperative (NSLC) Clearinghouse
www.nicsl.coled.umn.edu/

The NSLC Clearinghouse is a central repository of information about service-learning programs, organizations, people, calendar events, and literature/multimedia materials. The Clearinghouse provides access to service-learning information through both its Web site and a toll-free telephone number (1-800-808-SERVE). The Web site links to other service-learning sites and also lists national and federal service-learning organizations.

The Partnerships in Education (PIE) Network: Creating Community Partnerships
http://pie.wednet.edu/index.html

PIE is a cooperative effort of school districts, businesses, and agencies working together for the benefit of youth in Clark County, Washington. The PIE Web site offers an interesting look at a network of businesses and schools that work together to create service-learning and school-to-work opportunities for students within and beyond school.

Tennessee Technological University, Department of History
www.tntech.edu:8080/www/acad/hist/oral.html

This Web site links to other sites that teach oral history concepts, list other oral history links and resources, and house history project archives.

"What Did You Do in the War, Grandma?"
An Oral History of Rhode Island Women during World War II
www.stg.brown.edu/projects/WWII_Women/tocCS.html

Written and developed by high school students, this online project includes interviews of thirty-six Rhode Island women who recalled their lives in the years before, during, and after World War II. The Web site gives access to twenty-six of the stories, with one available in Real Audio. A print version is available for purchase from The Rhode Island Historical Society, 110 Benevolent Street, Providence, RI 02906.

UNIT ONE: OUTLINE OF ACTIVITIES, MATERIALS, TOOLS AND SUGGESTED TIME

The following is an outline of activities for The Individual and the Community unit that details the materials, tools, and handouts that should be supplied to students as well as suggested time allotments for activities. Pencils, lined paper, and unlined paper are not included in the materials list, but will be needed for most activities. Time estimates are approximate and may vary considerably, depending on the needs of the particular group of students and the teacher/facilitator.

CityWorks Goal 1 Communicating Well

CITYWORKS GOAL 2 Working as a Team

CITYWORKS GOAL 3 Producing High-quality Work

CITYWORKS GOAL 4 Using Math, Measurement, and Fundamentals of Design

CITYWORKS GOAL 5 Using Problem-Solving Skills

CITYWORKS GOAL 6 Knowing Your Community's Resources and Needs

UNIT TWO: OUTLINE OF ACTIVITIES, MATERIALS, TOOLS AND SUGGESTED TIME

The following is an outline of activities for the WalkAbout the Community unit detailing the materials, tools and handouts that should be supplied to students as well as suggested time allotments for activities. Pencils, lined paper, and unlined paper are not included in the materials list, but will be needed for most activities. Time estimates are approximate and may vary considerably, depending on the needs of the particular group of students and the teacher/facilitator.

WalkAbout the Community Introduction (page 115)
SUGGESTED TIME ALLOTMENT: half hour to 1 hour for discussion of introduction and review of upcoming activities

What's a Neighborhood (page 115)
SUGGESTED TIME ALLOTMENT: 1-2 hours
MATERIALS: Map or maps of the city, colored pencils or markers, blackboard, or newsprint for recording brainstorm information

Neighborhood Report Card (pages 117)
SUGGESTED TIME ALLOTMENT: 1-2 hours

Symbols (pages 119)
Group Mapping Symbols
SUGGESTED TIME ALLOTMENT: half to 1 hour for Symbols handout and discussion, 1 hour for Individual Mapping Symbols, 1 hour for Group Mapping Symbols

Tour of Your Neighborhood (page 122)
SUGGESTED TIME ALLOTMENT: half to 1 hour

Mapping Your Block (page 123)
SUGGESTED TIME ALLOTMENT: 1 to 1-1/2 hours to draw map; Each student will most likely need to take field notes as homework

Group Neighborhood Presentation Board (page 123)
SUGGESTED TIME ALLOTMENT: 1 hour to create presentation board, 1-2 hours for individual student presentations and group discussion
MATERIALS: Poster or mat board, a map of the city, markers, and/or colored pencils, and a glue stick

Neighborhoods: WorkLog Reflection (page 124)
SUGGESTED TIME ALLOTMENT: 20 minutes to 1-1/2 hours (varies depending on teacher and students)
TOOLS: Access to computer for keyboarding if preferred

Investigating a Focus Theme (page 125)
SUGGESTED TIME ALLOTMENT: 1-2 hours for group discussion and brainstorming of possible focus themes

Choosing Your Focus Theme (pages 126)
SUGGESTED TIME ALLOTMENT: half hour to brainstorm each of three theme proposals, half hour to write each proposal

Final Study Plan for Focus Theme (page 135)
SUGGESTED TIME ALLOTMENT: 1 to 2 hours for group brainstorming and writing of final study plan and timeline
MATERIALS: Blackboard, or markers and newsprint for group brainstorming
Note: The research phase of the WalkAbout activity, which includes study area observations and mapping, may take anywhere from 15 to 30 hours, spaced over a period of 2 to 4 weeks.

Observing Your Study Area (pages 135)
SUGGESTED TIME ALLOTMENT: 1 to 1-1/2 hours for observation, writing, and group discussion

Observation Exercise: WorkLog Reflection (page 137)
SUGGESTED TIME ALLOTMENT: 20 minutes to 1-1/2 hours (varies depending on teacher and students)
TOOLS: Access to computer for keyboarding if preferred

Mapping Your Study Area (page 138)
SUGGESTED TIME ALLOTMENT: 1-2 hours for on-site mapping.
MATERIALS: For on-site mapping, street diagram for study area (either photocopied or transcribed from map), Group Mapping Symbols sheet for student reference, and clipboards. For final study area map: drawing paper, markers, and colored pens and pencils.
TOOLS AND EQUIPMENT: For final study area map: Architectural scale, triangles, and other drafting tools as needed

Presentation Boards (pages 139)
SUGGESTED TIME ALLOTMENT: 6-12 hours for assembling, editing, keyboarding, drawing, and laying out information to go on presentation boards
MATERIALS: Poster or mat boards (assorted colors), drawing paper, colored pens and pencils, markers, glue sticks, duct tape (for attaching boards together), and Polaroid film
TOOLS AND EQUIPMENT: Access to computer for keyboarding, mat knives, straight-edged metal rulers, and Polaroid camera(s)

Research Methods: WorkLog Reflection (page 141)
SUGGESTED TIME ALLOTMENT: 20 minutes to 1-1/2 hours (varies depending on teacher and students)
TOOLS: Access to computer for keyboarding if preferred

WalkAbout: WorkLog Reflection (page 141)
SUGGESTED TIME ALLOTMENT: 20 minutes to 1-1/2 hours (varies depending on teacher and students)
TOOLS: Access to computer for keyboarding if preferred

WalkAbout: Portfolio Record Form (page 142)
SUGGESTED TIME ALLOTMENT: 1/2 hour to 1 hour for rough draft, 1/2 hour for copying onto Portfolio Record form.
MATERIALS: Lined paper for rough draft

Putting it all Together for Your Portfolio (page 145)
SUGGESTED TIME ALLOTMENT: 4-8 hours, or as needed for getting up to date on Personal Statement, Resumé, WorkLog reflections, Portfolio Record forms, and for putting together other samples of work for inclusion in the portfolio binder
MATERIALS: Portfolio binder packet, portfolio three-ring binder, blank WorkLog and Portfolio Record forms, drawing paper, colored pens and markers, and glue sticks.
TOOLS AND EQUIPMENT: Three-hole punch and any other tools needed for completing work samples

UNIT THREE: OUTLINE OF ACTIVITIES, MATERIALS, TOOLS AND SUGGESTED TIME

The following is an outline of activities for the Contributing to the Community unit describing the materials, tools, and handouts that should be supplied to students as well as suggested time allotments for activities. Pencils, lined paper, and unlined paper are not included in the materials list but will be needed. Time estimates are approximate and may vary considerably, depending on the needs of the particular group of students and the teacher/facilitator.

Introduction (page 149)
SUGGESTED TIME ALLOTMENT: 1/2 hour to 1 hour for discussion of introduction and review of upcoming activities

What is Community Development? (page 150)
SUGGESTED TIME ALLOTMENT: 1 hour for preparation of questions for representatives from the city's Office of Community Development; 1 to 3 hours for presentation
MATERIALS: Newsprint and markers for brainstorming lists and masking tape for hanging lists (although blackboards may be used, newsprint creates a more permanent record of ideas)

Creating a Neighborhood Resources and Needs Booklet (page 151)
SUGGESTED TIME ALLOTMENT: 5-10 hours
MATERIALS: 8-1/2" x 11" cover stock (assorted colors) for booklet covers, Polaroid film (if possible), community brochures and newspapers, colored pencils and pens, drawing paper
TOOLS AND EQUIPMENT: Polaroid camera (if possible); access to computer for keyboarding

Neighborhood Resources and Needs: WorkLog Reflection (page 185)
SUGGESTED TIME ALLOTMENT: 20 minutes to 1-1/2 hours (varies depending on teacher and students)
TOOLS: Access to computer for keyboarding if preferred

The Phases of the CityWorks Community Development Project

Project Identification Phase (page 154)
SUGGESTED TIME ALLOTMENT: 3-6 hours for reviewing examples of umbrella themes listed in curriculum and brainstorming ideas for umbrella themes and specific small-group projects
MATERIALS: Newsprint and markers for brainstorming lists and masking tape for hanging lists (although blackboards may be used, newsprint creates a more permanent record of ideas)

Research and Investigation Phase (page 155)

SUGGESTED TIME ALLOTMENT: 15-30 hours spaced over three to six weeks
MATERIALS (depending on projects): Polaroid film, drawing paper, and cassette tapes for interviews
TOOLS AND EQUIPMENT (depending on projects): Clipboards, Polaroid cameras, hand-held tape recorders for interviews

Production Phase (page 156)

SUGGESTED TIME ALLOTMENT: 20-40 hours spaced over 4-8 weeks
MATERIALS (depending on projects): Polaroid film, drawing paper, poster and/or mat boards (assorted colors), glue sticks, white glue, glue gun sticks, chip board (for model making), construction paper (assorted colors), colored markers and pens, duct tape (for attaching contiguous mat boards), and any other materials needed for layout and construction of presentations boards and models
TOOLS AND EQUIPMENT (depending on projects): Polaroid cameras, access to computers for keyboarding and graphics, and assorted drafting and model-making tools (architectural scales, utility knives, metal straight-edged rulers, and glue guns).

Exhibition Phase (page 157)

SUGGESTED TIME ALLOTMENT: 2-5 hours for preparation and practice of presentations, 2-5 hours for presentations (depending on number of groups presenting)
MATERIALS: Poster board for signage, colored markers and pens, materials for hanging exhibit work (tape, duct tape, push pins, picture-hanging hooks), and videotapes (for taping practice presentations and actual presentations)
TOOLS AND EQUIPMENT: Microphone system (if necessary for presentations); video camera (for taping practice presentations and actual presentations); and VCRs and video monitors for any video work being presented

Researching Your Project: WorkLog Reflection (page 166)

SUGGESTED TIME ALLOTMENT: 20 minutes to 1-1/2 hours (varies depending on teacher and students)
TOOLS: Access to computer for keyboarding if preferred

Contributing to the Community: WorkLog Reflection (page 167)

SUGGESTED TIME ALLOTMENT: 20 minutes to 1-1/2 hours (varies depending on teacher and students)
TOOLS: Access to computer for keyboarding if preferred

Contributing to the Community - Portfolio Record Form (page 168)

SUGGESTED TIME ALLOTMENT: 1/2 hour to 1 hour for rough draft; 1/2 hour for copying onto Portfolio Record form
MATERIALS: Lined paper for rough draft

Putting It All Together for Your Portfolio (page 170)

SUGGESTED TIME ALLOTMENT: 4-8 hours, or as needed for getting up to date on Personal Statement, Resumé, WorkLog reflections, Portfolio Record forms, and for putting together other samples of work for inclusion in the portfolio binder
MATERIALS: Portfolio binder packet, portfolio three-ring binder, blank WorkLog and Portfolio Record forms, drawing paper, colored pens and markers, and glue sticks
TOOLS AND EQUIPMENT: Three-hole punch and any other tools needed for completing work samples

The following pages contain the front and back sides of blank Work-Log reflection, Portfolio Record, and Record of Accomplishment forms. The WorkLog forms should be photocopied and used for all WorkLog reflection activities. The Portfolio Record form blanks can be photocopied and used for "free write" portfolio records of student work, although each Portfolio Record activity in this curriculum comes with its own Portfolio Record form with specific questions pertaining to the activity.

NAME

DATE

THEME

WORK
LOG

NAME

DATE

THEME

PORTFOLIO RECORD

NAME

DATE

THEME

RECORD OF ACCOMPLISHMENT

In CityWorks students develop and practice important skills and personal qualities required for success in the world today. Below is a list of the six CityWorks goals. Describe selected examples of work you have completed that illustrate or pertain to each of these goals.

1. Communicating Well:

2. Working as a Team:

3. Producing High Quality Work:

4. Using Math, Measurement, and the Fundamentals of Design:

5. Using Problem-Solving Skills:

6. Knowing Your Community's Resources and Needs: